The Macat Library

世界思想宝库钥匙丛书

解析米歇尔·福柯

《规训与惩罚》

AN ANALYSIS OF

MICHEL FOUCAULT'S

DISCIPLINE AND PUNISH

Meghan Kallman   Rachele Dini ◎ 著

余畅 ◎ 译

上海外语教育出版社
外教社 SHANGHAI FOREIGN LANGUAGE EDUCATION PRESS

MACAT

目　录

CONTENTS

引言

要 点

- 米歇尔·福柯（1926—1984）是法国社会哲学家、历史学家。

- 《规训与惩罚》通过追溯现代监狱的历史及现代监狱对医院、工厂、学校和工作场所等其他社会机构的影响，提出现代权力（社会各个群体所掌握的权力）关系理论。

- 《规训与惩罚》研究监视*（系统性监控）和知识生产在个体建构和关系构建中所扮演的角色，由此影响了人文社科学者对于权力概念的解读。

米歇尔·福柯其人

米歇尔·福柯是《规训与惩罚：监狱的诞生》（1975）的作者，他是法国激进派社会哲学家、历史学家和文学评论家。如今，他被公认为社会科学和人文科学领域最富影响力的当代思想家之一。

福柯在法国西部的一个富庶而保守的家庭里长大，其父为外科医生，因此他从小就受到了良好的教育。在大学时期，福柯违背了父亲的意愿，选择学习哲学*和科学史，他的博士论文则研究疯癫史。在其博士论文中，他区分了精神病和疯癫，强调后者是基于主观假设的社会建构。

这篇论文后来被翻译成英语出版成书，书名为《疯癫与文明》，后改为《疯癫史》。该书广受好评，并获得法国国家科学研究中心颁发的金奖，该中心是法国最重要的政府研究机构。福柯随后发表了《临床医学的诞生》（1963）、《词与物》（1966）和《知识考古学》（1969）等专著。

福柯一生致力于左翼政治活动：例如，他曾是带头反对监狱制度的激进分子。20 世纪六七十年代的许多法国左翼激进主义运动深受马克思主义 * 思想的影响。根据德国政治理论家卡尔·马克思 * 著作中的观点，废止剥削雇佣劳动者和其他劳动者的权力机制是必要的。然而，福柯对思想界的贡献，在于他主张权力并不为个体或某个团体所独有：个体由其所处的权力关系构建而成，因而无法超脱其外。

《规训与惩罚》的主要内容

在《规训与惩罚》中，福柯颠覆了对权力的传统界定，不认同权力由政府、国王或是财阀单向施加于个体之上的观点。在福柯看来，权力即为"规训"*。关注福柯如何解读该术语，尤其重要；对福柯而言，规训并非自上而下式的直接胁迫 *，而是通过权力运作促使个体自我规训。

以刑罚制度为例，福柯论证了自 17 世纪监狱问世以来，监狱的规训如何作为特殊的权力形式扎根于社会体系之中。换言之，监狱作为规训机构的出现是某种"历史偶然性"*，即监狱的规训效应产生于特定的历史语境中。

除了研究这类规训过程的发展史，福柯还关注运用此类规训手法的权力的运作策略和机制。在本书中，福柯深入探讨了肉体、个体和所谓"权力—知识"*[1] 三者之间的关系，其笔下的"权力—知识"是指权力和知识的结合，使得掌权阶层得以划分和控制群众和事物。以上都是在其著作中重复出现的主题。

《规训与惩罚》一书认为，社会机构通过凝视 *——即"注视"[2] 将权力和规训施加于社会主体的肉体和心灵之上。基于此论断，福柯转而讨论全景式监狱 *，此概念是 18 世纪晚期英国社会改革家杰里米·边沁*构想的一种监狱模型。在全景式监狱中，因犯无法看到看守人员，因此无从知晓自己是否正在被监视；正是这种时刻都被监视的可能性促使因犯们好好表现。福柯指出，全景敞视建筑及其背后蕴含的权力运作机制不但被运用到监狱设计上，还被应用于其他社会机构中（譬如，当一个司机不能断定自己是否正在被超速摄像头追踪时，"以防万一"，他/她可能不会超速）。据此观点，当个体意识到自身可能受到控制，其表现会受到制约。

在福柯看来，个体在本质上是此类监视和控制下的产物。政府机构的监视——即系统性监控——造就了"驯顺的肉体"[3]。福柯将"驯顺的肉体"定义为被监控、被精神控制，紧接着被训练成自我管理的人体。简言之，出于对被监视、被评估或是被惩罚的畏惧，我们避免做某些事情，而我们的个性也由此被限定。

《规训与惩罚》的学术价值

《规训与惩罚》被公认为是探讨社会学、历史学和哲学思想的现代经典著作之一。福柯在其有关社会体制的研究中，对权力进行了颠覆性解析，充分阐明了个体和群体如何被统治。福柯在书中追溯了现代权力结构——譬如当下的监狱体系——的演变以及现代权力机构对于人类自由和个体身份的影响。《规训与惩罚》一书的独到之处也在于其研究路径：与其说该书是关于权力的理论研究，不如说该书考察了权力的演变史。福柯的史学研究路径可以用来研究各色各样的机构和权力结构；其著作本身并非旨在批判某一特定体系，而是为了更好地理解权力自身如何运作。

福柯的分析促使学者们极大地改变了先前对权力运作机制、知识的概念和个体构成方式的认知。尽管有些社会学家可能不认同福柯对于权力的解读，但受过专业训练的社会学家都熟悉福柯的著作。

《规训与惩罚》的影响也扩散到了其他学科领域。福柯提出，个体被其所处的权力和知识体系所塑造；这一观点被广泛运用于有关人类能动性和选择能力的学术论争以及关于个体身份的讨论中。福柯式权力概念和其他概念，诸如话语＊（福柯界定的"话语"是指在历史和权力的双重作用下出现的某种言说方式——但这一术语往往被用来指称思想交流，以及这种交流方式如何界定了人们对于某些事物的理解）、"权力—知识"⁴和全景敞视主义＊（即全景式监狱为社会中所有权力关系提供了模型的理论），不仅成为社会学＊术语的一部分，还出现在历史学、经济学＊、人类学＊和政治科学＊等学科中。

文化研究＊、媒体研究＊和文学研究＊领域的学者也运用福柯的观点解析文学、音乐、电影和电视作品中的权力关系。《规训与惩罚》一书中所提出的理论，经常被用来解释个体如何使权力内化，以及权力的内化对于社会关系和抵抗的可能性的影响。

在当下关于数字时代个人隐私的讨论中，福柯的思想有了新的意义。福柯觉察到社会机构的监控带来的实际效益以及随之产生的人道代价，他的这一认知是我们当下进行的诸多讨论的先声，包括"闭路电视（CCTV）＊摄像头的监控对我们的生活所产生的影响"这类问题。同样的，2013年"吹哨人"爱德华·斯诺登＊披露了美国国家安全局（NSA）＊对于美国公民的监听事实，这一事件也多方面印证了福柯的某些论点。

1. 米歇尔·福柯:《规训与惩罚：监狱的诞生》，纽约州谢里登：温特吉出版社，1979 年，第 27 页。
2. 福柯:《规训与惩罚》，第 96 页。
3. 福柯:《规训与惩罚》，第 135 页。
4. 福柯:《规训与惩罚》，第 27 页。

第一部分：学术渊源

1 作者生平与历史背景

要点 ⚏━

- 米歇尔·福柯的这本著作凭借其对"权力"的新颖解读，已经成为诸多学科的重要读本。对于相关议题中出现的新焦点，诸如国家对于公共区域和互联网的监视，该书仍具有影响力。

- 福柯的观点受其早年经历的影响，尤其是他压抑的成长过程（其同性恋身份）、在法国精神病院以及身为监狱改革小组一员的亲身经历。

- 福柯曾参与法国极左翼政治活动和 1968 年"五月风暴"，这些活动深刻影响了法国的社会思潮，也帮助塑造了福柯的思想观念。

为何要读这部著作？

米歇尔·福柯的《规训与惩罚：监狱的诞生》（1975）是许多学科的重要读本，包括社会学（研究社会史和社会结构的学科）、哲学（研究关于现实、知识和存在等人类根本性问题的学科）和历史学。本书以独特的视角分析了权力演变和现代权力结构，并以此为思路启发读者重新审视我们对于权力本质、理智和个体构成等概念的惯常理解。

历史学家、犯罪学家（研究犯罪及犯罪行为的学者）和哲学家们仍将《规训与惩罚》视为重要读本——他们或认同福柯在该书中所表述的史学研究观点，或支持其提出的有关现代监狱演变和运作的理论，或认可其在书中论及的理智和理性 * 的本质。同时，又因福柯在书中以新颖的视角重新阐释了现代权力的本质，各学科领域中对权力概念感兴趣的学者都仍在阅读该书。加之学界围绕权力、理智的本质、惩罚在社会中所扮演的角色以及惩罚的形式等相关问题的研究历久不衰，《规训与惩罚》一书短期内仍将具有重大意义。对于使用乃至滥用监测技术的担忧，包括公共场所监控摄像头的泛滥以及网络监控＊（即对互联网使用的监控）的出现，福柯的著作将获得新的意义。

> "我不是在个人问题上找麻烦；我认为个人问题不成问题。"
>
> —— 米歇尔·福柯：《乔姆斯基—福柯论辩录》

作者生平

米歇尔·福柯（1926—1984）出生于法国一个富庶而保守的家庭。他的父亲是外科医生，殷切期望福柯能子承父业。然而福柯违背父亲的意志，选择去巴黎一所有名的公立学校——亨利四世中学学习哲学。在那里，他师从让·伊波利特＊，一位研究 19 世纪哲学家黑格尔＊的专家。1946 年，福柯考入巴黎高等师范学院（ENS）。在这所法国最负盛名的人文类院校中，他受到了马克思主义哲学家路易·阿尔都塞＊的影响。1948 年，福柯获得第一个心理学学位；1951 年获得第二个哲学学位。他与同样著名的哲学家莫里斯·梅洛-庞蒂＊共事，梅洛-庞蒂因其现象学＊著作而闻名（大体说来，现象学是一种哲学研究路径，强调知觉在意识构成中所处的位置和所扮演的角色）。

终其职业生涯，福柯承认自己的亲身经历对其作品产生了极大的影响——特别是他的性取向以及他在精神病院和监狱系统的亲身经历。作为一个同性恋，福柯早年被压抑的性别身份使其怀有负罪感。1948 年，福柯尝试自杀失败，随后在巴黎接受精神治疗。根据医生的诊断，福柯之所以数次企图自杀，是出于他公开自己同性恋身份的羞愧感；在当时的法国社会，同性恋被视为祸害。

福柯关注权力、疯癫和性，这些主题在其著作中反复出现。他的首部著作——《疯癫与文明》（1961）论及精神病学*；这是与其经历密切相关的学科，因为他曾是接受心理治疗的病人，同时又在 20 世纪 50 年代担任一家精神病院的研究员。福柯最早获得的两个学位分属心理学*和现象学，因此其著作的理论视角和研究路径始终带有这两门学科的烙印。此外，福柯的社会身份及其对被压迫者的关注也贯穿其作品始终。

到了 20 世纪 70 年代初期，福柯积极涉足政治领域。他协助成立了监狱信息小组，旨在引导媒体和大众关注监狱条件。这段时间政治激进主义的出现以及福柯有关规训制度著作的发表，都为《规训与惩罚》的最终诞生创造了条件。

创作背景

福柯创作《规训与惩罚》期间，正值 20 世纪 60 年代法国社会文化剧变和政治动荡时期。在当时，法国社会出现了一系列冲突，包括对法国介入越南战争*（指 1955 年至 1975 年间发生在老挝、柬埔寨和越南的战争）的声讨、对法国在殖民地所作所为（和对殖民*体系）的抗议以及对法国教育体系的不满——批评家们抨击教育体系，指责该体系只保障富人的孩子受教育后可以谋得最好的职位。与此同时，法国社会反资本主义情绪高涨，全国范围内都出现了罢工以及占领学校和工厂的行为。

1968 年的"五月风暴"*标志着此次骚动的高潮：高校学生占领了欧洲最著名的院校之一——巴黎索邦大学，抵制资本主义制度和"传统"价值观；同时，共计 1 100 万工人参与这场为期两周的大罢工，期间法国经济几近瘫痪。甚至在法国总统秘密潜逃的数小时内，政府机构停止运转。这一历史阶段深刻影响了法国社会，常被视为一个重要的转折点。

这一历史语境对于理解福柯作品的起源至关重要：作为一名学者，福柯也积极投身于各类左翼运动。他参与反殖民主义运动，在阿尔及利亚战争（1954—1962）*中，他支持阿尔及利亚摆脱法国殖民统治以赢得独立。他也参与了 20 世纪 60 年代的反传统精神病学运动*，该运动旨在反对某些精神病疗法，包括电击疗法和脑白质切除术（如今仍备受诟病的一种精神病疗法，该疗法包括切除部分大脑前额叶）。此外，他还支持 1978 年爆发的伊朗伊斯兰革命*，并在意大利《晚邮报》和法国新闻杂志《新观察家》上撰文声援。然而，福柯并非关注某一党派的政治利益，而是权力机制的运作。福柯对于此次革命的关注点，在于该革命在削弱和去除前伊朗政权和权力方面所发挥的作用，而不在于取代伊朗君主制的新政体。

福柯对于殖民压迫、极权主义*（一种政治体系，在这种体系下，公民完全听命于国家权力）和精神病疗法的批判与其关于性压抑和"权力—知识"复合体（指掌握权力的上层控制信息或知识生产的方式）的观点紧密相关。表面看来，《规训与惩罚》是在讲述现代监狱和现代惩罚方式的演变史，但同时它还是一部批判现代社会迫使个体自我规训和遵从标准的著作。

2 学术背景

要点 🔑

- 福柯生活的时代，正值存在主义*和现象学的哲学研究路径以及马克思主义学派的经济社会分析方法在左翼思想中占主导地位。福柯挑战以上观点，并转向后结构主义*思想，认为人类身份是在社会和历史中建构的。

- 福柯抨击法国知名哲学家让－保罗·萨特*，认为他过分关注个体而忽视了更为宽泛的社会制度对于个体身份的塑造。

- 受德国哲学家弗里德里希·尼采*的影响，福柯认为理性、惩罚和权力都不是一成不变的观念，相反，这些观念脱胎于任何特定社会的历史。

著作语境

福柯将《规训与惩罚》称为"现代灵魂的演变史"。[1] 该书的思想与当时主导左翼政治思潮的马克思主义理论以及结构主义理论*（结构主义分析人类经验和文化，考察形成此种经验和文化的意识形态构架、社会文化构成和经济结构）背道而驰。福柯青年时期深受法国社会的主导哲学思潮影响，包括存在主义（一种哲学研究路径，强调个体经验和个体特质）、现象学（主要研究知觉在意识构成中所处的位置和所扮演的角色）和马克思主义（关于社会和政治进程的学说，该学说主要建立在对资本主义的批判性分析之上）。这三大思潮的纽带是它们各自的"人道主义"*内核，特别是它们一致认为人类行为由人性和阶级或社会不平等决定，而非遵照上帝指示产生。

20 世纪五六十年代，以上三种思潮受到结构主义的挑战。结构主义理论认为人类的行为和思想是通过语言媒介而被社会建构。结构主义者认为，我们对特定事件、时刻、人物和活动的理解完全基于我们的信仰体系、所处历史语境、文化背景和语言。福柯在此观点上更进一步。他的观点更接近于后结构主义*，即认为个体身份和个体价值并非一成不变，而是取决于个体境遇和思维视角（即看待事物所采取的立场）。

后结构主义者主张文本也可以用同样的方式理解。文本意义取决于客观环境、阅读视角和历史时期。一本书、一场政治演讲或是一个文本可以有多种解读方式，而这些解读方式的选择完全取决于读者。循此思路，福柯指出知识和身份都是由社会建构的：它们并非天然存在的，而是社会准则、信仰或是风俗的产物。这一观点也可以用来理解监狱体系，监狱同样不是社会固有的基本组成部分，而是可变的社会惯例。

> "'启蒙'，在发现自由的同时，也发明了规训。"
>
> —— 米歇尔·福柯：《规训与惩罚：监狱的诞生》

学科概览

对以上所提及的思想流派做出最大贡献的哲学家，要数莫里斯·梅洛-庞蒂和让-保罗·萨特。与其说这些思想家的作品塑造了福柯的研究，不如说他们的作品塑造了福柯的研究领域。不过，他们所秉持的一些观点最终被福柯摈弃。按照梅洛-庞蒂的思路，福柯关注个体、主体性和身体经验，并强调此种经验对于理解政治和社会世界的重要性。梅洛-庞蒂的哲学考察身体、身体认知和感受世界的方式，以及身体如何赋予感知以秩序和意义，借此把握人类普遍境遇。然而，福柯反对人类经验的普遍性一说。

萨特的作品也为福柯的学术成长和哲学路径择取提供了重要思想资源。萨特和福柯都同情边缘人群，包括少数民族、同性恋群体和罪犯。此种同情心促使他们倒向政治激进主义。即便如此，福柯并未受到萨特哲学著作的影响，反而常常反驳萨特的观点。虽然他们有些观点一致，但是对他们的研究应当分而视之，甚至可以看作彼此对立。福柯批判萨特对于个体经验的强调，斥之为"超验自恋"。福柯之所以这么说，是因为他认为萨特过度强调个体的重要性，而忽视了个体身处的多重体系。"超验自恋"这一冒犯性言语，是福柯对萨特"视个体为社会体系中心"这一观点的抨击；在福柯看来，个体是被社会体系建构的。

由于反对人类普遍性一说，福柯的观点被视作近似结构主义和后结构主义理论。结构主义理论与福柯观点的相似之处在于，它们都关注个体如何以语言为媒介发展自身特质。而后结构主义思想认为可以用多种方式解读文本或行为等实体，这一观点与福柯对于知识和知识体系运作的理解异曲同工，福柯认为知识和知识体系可以被塑造，并且延伸到各个领域。

学术渊源

尽管福柯的思想来源极其多元，但毋庸置疑的是，结构主义、后结构主义以及19世纪德国哲学家弗里德里希·尼采的思想对他有很大的影响。

福柯指出监狱的演变是更为宽泛的社会结构和历史运作的结

果，这一解读表明他受到了结构主义思想的影响。结构主义思想认为，社会机构（例如学校或法律体系）塑造了个体身份。福柯并未将监狱机构或是个体的存在视为理所应当，相反，他更关注它们是如何被创造的。从福柯贯穿全书的主张可以看出，他所受到的后结构主义影响，即福柯认为刑罚制度有多重意义：既可以产生积极效应，也可以充满压迫性。

但福柯认为自己不属于以上任何一个流派。他强调自身所受到的主要影响源自尼采著作中所采用的方法论，即"谱系学"*，这也是书中最值得称道的地方。由此可以明显看出尼采对福柯思想的影响，特别是尼采有关道德的学说。福柯的"知识考古学"[2]研究直接引用了尼采"道德的谱系"[3]这一概念。尼采并没有将道德视作先定的存在，而是试图发掘我们的价值观和道德观如何在历史语境中被塑造。

尼采的研究方法影响了福柯在《规训与惩罚》一书中的观点。福柯在书中指出：我们对于自启蒙运动*（欧洲思想史上的重要阶段，时间跨度约为 1650 年至 1780 年，相对于宗教和迷信，这一时期更强调理性思想和行为）流传至今的诸如理性、惩罚和权力等观念的认知同样是历史偶然性的产物，我们可以追溯这些观念的演变过程。

谱系学可以被视作一种研究范式，即试图通过回溯过去以解释当下，试图追溯我们如何从"那里"到达"这里"。对福柯而言，正是谱系学研究路径促使其洞察规训和权力的本质，以及这两者如何建构个体。

1. 米歇尔·福柯:《规训与惩罚：监狱的诞生》，纽约州谢里登：温特吉出版社，1979 年，第 23 页。
2. 福柯:《规训与惩罚》，第 27 页。
3. 弗里德里希·威廉·尼采:《论道德的谱系》，伦敦和纽约：麦克米伦出版社，1897 年。

3 主导命题

要点 🔑

- 福柯的作品指出：适当行为的衡量标准、理性和权力的行使都是特定历史语境的产物，并且这三者随着时间的推移而不断变化。

- 福柯的研究方法触怒了许多哲学家，在他们看来，哲学的目的在于找寻普世真理。

- 福柯试图论证与过去相比，现代社会中的权力已经进化，控制和惩罚"不良"行为的方式更难以觉察，且无处不在。然而，对于"我们已经稳步迈向更加理性的制度"这一普遍观点，福柯并不赞同。

核心问题

在《规训与惩罚》中，福柯尝试了解现代个体的形成方式以及现代权力形式与旧权力形式的区别。他的研究不仅描述特定现代权力形式，还解释此种权力的形成过程。

福柯的研究集中考察人体和权力之间不断变化的关系；他认为，此种不断变化的关系从整体上影响了权力运作。从前，惩罚通过公共酷刑、甚至死刑等方式被施加于肉体之上；而如今，身体受制于准则、校正制度和规章条例。福柯关注个体如何成为权力的目标和产物；而这是通过规约个体行为的行为准则实现的。

福柯想借此说明权力和知识之间的关系。打个比方，机构权力——如学校和司法系统的权力——与知识建构息息相关；而且在福柯看来，这两者共同塑造了个体欲望，影响了个体认知自身在世界上所处位置的方式。福柯试图证明，每一个社会中被视作理所当然的准则或冲动都是特定历史语境的产物，并受制于建构它的知识体系。权力的运作依赖于制定衡量"正常"行为的准则。个体希望被视作"正常人"，因此他们便遵守这些准则。

> "不相应地建构一种知识领域就不可能有权力关系，不同时预设和建构权力关系也就不会有任何知识。"
>
> —— 米歇尔·福柯：《规训与惩罚：监狱的诞生》

参与者

不同于其他研究机构或社会结构的学者，福柯自称思想体系史学家。他的分析单位是塑造社会现实的语言；本质上，福柯试图理解语言和思维如何塑造出不同的思想体系。这是一种解读历史的全新视角，引导着福柯走进一个未知领域。

福柯的研究方法激怒了很多哲学家，因为哲学主要研究的问题向来被认为是探讨普遍真理——即研究适用于任何时间和空间的知识。从这个角度而言，哲学被视作独立于历史和文化之外的存在。福柯不同意此观点，他将语言和思想放置到特定社会、文化和历史语境中去研究。福柯招致的最强烈批评来自那些反对这种理论预设的批评家们。

福柯的批判者中最有名的要数德国社会学家尤尔根·哈贝马斯*。此外，他同样受到马克思主义哲学家们的强烈抨击，他们从唯物主义*角度解读权力，视权力为社会不公和财富分配不均的产物。这些马克思主义哲学家包括西蒙娜·德·波伏娃*和存在主义者*让-保罗·萨特；波伏娃以其对女权主义*理论的贡献而著称，而萨特则视福柯先前的著作《词与物》（1966）为抨击马克思主义及其相关领域的右翼作品。萨特所指的相关领域包括现象学 *（一种哲学研究路径，考察知觉在意识构成中所处的位置和所扮演的角色）和存在主义（一种认为个体是意义建构的基础的哲学研究路径）。

当时的论战

福柯追随他的老师——哲学家让·伊波利特的步伐，反对当时风靡的对理性的经典解读。和伊波利特一样，福柯强调思想体系的多元性以及历史语境的重要性。《规训与惩罚》提出，理性是特定历史语境下的产物（即对理性的解读取决于特定历史时期的时代观念），而福柯在该书中对权力的解读是论证此哲学论点的关键。循此思路，在某个时代被视作合理的、理性的或是合逻辑的行为到了另一个时代就可能被认作是不合理的、不理性的或是不合逻辑的。福柯尤其不满"人类已经向理性稳步发展"这一观点。他再现了惩罚的演变过程——从绞刑架之类的恐怖场景演变到采用各类强制性手段来控制和校正行为的机构体系。由此，福柯质疑"人类向着更高层次的理性稳步前行"这一观点。

福柯对权力运作方式的看法（即认为权力运作是通过建构有关个体的"知识"来实现）迥异于当时在法国风靡的左翼马克思主义学派的唯物主义权力论。福柯将权力视作"毛细血管"，[2] 即认为权力总是无处不在，甚至渗透到日常生活的方方面面。他对于权力的解读与马克思主义计量经济 *分析（对经济统计数据的解读）的权力截然相反，计量经济分析认为权力根植于经济剥削和权贵自上而下施加的权威之中。

1. 迪迪埃·埃里蓬:《米歇尔·福柯及其同时代人》,巴黎:法雅出版社,1994年,第155—186页。

2. 米歇尔·福柯:《规训与惩罚:监狱的诞生》,纽约州谢里登:温特吉出版社,1979年,第198页。

4 作者贡献

要点 ✪━━

- 米歇尔·福柯在《规训与惩罚》中考察了 18 世纪监狱系统及其向现代刑罚体系的演变进程，以追溯现代权力关系史。

- 在福柯看来，权力通过"权力—知识"模式运作，这一模式将个体进行分类，并且通过规训手段调节个体的身体在时间和空间上的行为。

- 福柯同时代的马克思主义思想家认为权力以经济基础和阶级地位为基石，但福柯并不认同这一观点，他更关注语言和权力机制。

作者目标

在离世前不久接受的一系列访谈中，福柯谈及《规训与惩罚：监狱的诞生》一书时表示，他撰写此书的根本目的在于理解现代权力关系史，而非创建关于权力的理论。[1] 经济学家和政治理论家卡尔·马克思在著作中指出，谁掌控经济大权谁就掌控权力；经济因素决定谁享有权力。然而，在福柯看来，权力是基础性的，且不由经济地位决定。在马克思主义政治经济学分析中，权力被用来镇压反抗或是禁止行动；而在福柯的著作中，权力具有建构效应：权力建构了个体，也建构了社会对于这些个体身份的解读。

《规训与惩罚》的宗旨是追溯 18 世纪监狱体系所蕴含的权力运作模式。福柯旨在通过溯源 18 世纪监狱体系研究理性、身体以及当时进行的"何为理性和正义"的讨论，并追溯以上观念从 18 世纪演变至今的历史。监狱体系背后的权力关系有助于我们理解个体建构，这反过来又能帮助我们理解权力如何运作以及权力为何生效。

通过探讨以上观点，福柯批判了以理性为中心的启蒙思想和描述知识在历史语境中的建构方式，颠覆了社会学家们所理解的权力和理性。

> "我并非在创建有关权力的理论。我是在研究特定时期加诸自我之上的自我的自反性的建构方式以及与之相关的真理话语的演变史。当我谈论 18 世纪的监禁制度时，我指的是存在于那个时期的权力关系。"
>
> —— 米歇尔·福柯，载《批判与权力：重铸福柯和哈贝马斯之争》

研究方法

福柯对惩罚的研究集中在三个相互关联的主要概念上：权力、知识和身体，他强调这三者是任何政权的基石。

福柯向来以界定权力**不是**什么，而非权力**是**什么而闻名；然而，值得一提的是，在福柯看来，权力并不能被人所占有，而只能在社会关系中生成和运作。个体并不拥有或持有权力，而是行使权力。即便是在最微小的互动中，都会有权力运作。权力不同于冲突或公开统治。权力更具有生产性；它通过个体运作，并塑造个体，而并不与个体的自然意志或先存意志相冲突。

值得注意的是，《规训与惩罚》并不关注与特定政治活动或特定群体相关的权力运作，而是关注权力如何在现代社会中运作，以及此种权力机制的由来。

福柯描述了权力的运作策略如何取决于对其目标群体的"了解"。为了控制某物或某人，就需要掌握有关他们的"知识"。这里提到的"了解"和"知识",是指将个体划分为几类。比方说,中学和大学记录学生的成绩。通过此举,它们将年轻学子划分为"A""B""C"三个等级,从而建构有关学生个体的"知识"。受学校对成绩等级划分的影响,学生会努力学习以挣得 A 等,而不选择去竞争 B 等。中学或大学通过这种方法向学生施加权力控制。由此看来,权力和知识密不可分、相互依存。福柯提出的术语"权力—知识"[2]正是强调了这种关联。

最后,福柯认为"权力—知识"的重点运作对象是人体。制度造就了"驯顺的肉体"[3],这类个体通过自我规训来达到相应的标准。例如,士兵遵循一定的章法行走、谈话和站立,并通过此类身体动作表明他已达到部队给出的标准。

福柯认为权力通过规训机制运作。这里"规训"的含义不同于它的常用义。它指的是一种权力运作机制,即通过种种方式将权力施加于个体之上,以规训个体。规训可以在空间层面进行,例如,将他们关押进一幢建筑物中的某个特定房间或小牢房中;规训也可以在时间层面进行,例如给他们设定时刻表,限定他们全天的活动。福柯仔细地将规训与权力和惩罚加以区分,指出规训并不是我们惯常所理解的权力或惩罚,而是一种权力运作方式。

从上述这些观点出发,福柯将惩罚史视作社会关系网的演变史,这种关系网在"权力—知识"体制和人体之间的互动中慢慢形成。

时代贡献

尽管福柯的著作常常与结构主义、现象学和马克思主义理论联系在一起,但在《规训与惩罚》中,他的研究路径不同于这三个学派。相较于同时代的马克思主义学者的作品，福柯作品的不同之处在于他并非从经济学视角审视权力，也没有考察各个社会阶层之间的关系。《规训与惩罚》一书自始至终关注的是学科结构，而非经济结构。同样的，福柯的谱系学是对现象学和结构主义研究的重大突破。

现象学和结构主义关注特定知识或信仰赖以生存的结构。福柯的谱系学路径并不致力于描述"知识"或信仰体系的内容，而是关注推动特定"知识"或信仰体系形成的背后机制。换言之，他关注"真理"如何被建构。福柯将这一过程及它的内部运作界定为"话语机制的权术"[5]，他试图借此概念来说明我们用于描绘事物的语言既是权力的产物，也是权力的源头。

1. 迈克尔·凯利等：《批判与权力：重铸福柯和哈贝马斯之争》，马萨诸塞州坎布里奇；伦敦：麻省理工学院出版社，1994 年，第 129 页。
2. 米歇尔·福柯：《规训与惩罚：监狱的诞生》，纽约州谢里登：温特吉出版社，1979 年，第 27 页。
3. 福柯：《规训与惩罚》，第 135 页。
4. 福柯：《规训与惩罚》，第 27 页。
5. 米歇尔·福柯：《权力／知识：谈话录及其他作品选集，1972—1977》，纽约：兰登书屋数字出版社，1980 年，第 118 页。

第二部分：学术思想

5 思想主脉

要点 ⚷━

- 福柯的《规训与惩罚》考察了现代监狱的出现如何反映出国家在整个社会中权力行使方式的变化。

- 福柯认为，从 18 世纪起，国家的惩罚机制便从过去对肉体的折磨羞辱慢慢转变为一种更巧妙的机制，这种机制时刻对个体行为进行控制和校正。

- 福柯拒绝效仿任何哲学流派。他的文字虽然晦涩难懂，但社会科学家们却引用了很多他独创的概念（如"权力—知识"）作为各自学术领域的专业词汇。福柯在社会科学领域的巨大影响力可见一斑。

核心主题

米歇尔·福柯的《规训与惩罚：监狱的诞生》考察了现代刑罚系统的发展与整个社会组织的关系。福柯认为，权力行使方式在 18 世纪发生的变化表明社会结构本身已经发生改变，从经常性施加于肉体的、公开的惩罚转变为一种控制和校正系统。他写道，监狱一出现便承担起让罪犯改头换面的使命；简言之，这是从以惩罚为主到以校正为主的一种转变。

这种转变对社会影响深远。为了证明这点，福柯考察了源于监狱的校正方法是如何向整个社会渗透，并被运用于学校、医院、甚至是社会科学本身的。他强调，今天我们所知的社会学和哲学，都滥觞于早期监狱的运转模式。从广义上来说，《规训与惩罚》的研究主题是权力的制度性转变，是规训体系在社会的形成，是此种新权力形式与各学科（包括福柯自己的研究领域）之间的关系。

这部著作还考察了现代权力机制的非人化*效应（即现代权力机制剥夺了个体作为人的地位，特别是此种机制基于这样一种假设，即对"不完全具备独立人格"的个体行使权力会更简单）。福柯旨在揭示我们是如何日复一日地自我规训，最终成为某类个体。

福柯认为，现代监狱的诞生造就了罪犯。随着监狱的出现，罪犯在社会中的生存方式与以往大不相同。首先，由于触犯法律的人被打上了"罪犯"的烙印，加之出狱后无技傍身，所以他们常常再次作案，陷入职业犯罪的模式。其次，更重要的是，福柯认为监狱制造了"罪犯个体"这一特殊社会群体，从而成为滋生罪犯的场所。

这便是认识论意义上的罪犯产生史。

认识论*研究的是知识的起源及其范畴，本书中的认识论指限定和界定罪犯的知识体系，也就是说，为了改造囚犯，从囚犯初次犯罪开始，追踪、评估、判断他们行为的所有方式。换言之，刑罚制度给罪犯贴上了可辨识的标签。人们对该群体的认知是：他们做了被社会认定为错误的事，并且社会采取了相应措施以防他们重蹈覆辙。福柯强调，将触犯法律的人贴上"罪犯"这一标签的行为是不人道的，因为这种做法将个人视为一串人口统计数字。

总而言之，从将个体视作"犯了罪的人"到将其视作"罪犯"这一过程，确实存在认知上的转变。

> "我从事的历史研究基本上只有一个对象，即现代性的发端。"
>
> —— 米歇尔·福柯，载《米歇尔·福柯，对话录》

思想探究

《规训与惩罚》开篇探讨了两种迥异的惩罚方式，福柯认为它们代表了各个时代的刑罚方式。他在书中写道，早期的惩罚方式以羞辱犯罪者的身体为目的；而现代的惩罚方式则是为了让罪犯回归"正常"，驯顺听话。

在第一个例子中，他生动地描述了一场死刑——1757 年，一个人因意图刺杀法国国王而被公开处决。他在众目睽睽之下被大卸八块，呈现了一场全程处于国家监督之下的暴力仪式。福柯将这种以羞辱犯罪者身体来惩罚犯罪的行为视为一种典型的旧式惩罚方式。

第二个例子是八十年后，巴黎一所少管所的作息时刻表。这套日程严格规定了所有犯人的生活作息，他们的所有活动，包括吃饭、睡觉、运动及洗漱，都必须按照规定的时间进行。在这个例子中，惩罚于悄无声息中进行，没有骇人的场面或仪式性酷刑。此举的宗旨不在于报复，而在于改造：即救赎犯罪者的灵魂。控制他们的行动及活动场所来最终改变他们的行为。

在福柯看来，控制体系从依赖暴力运作到依靠知识，这一转变本身颇具广泛而深远的影响。这类控制体系的手段和目的事实上象征了现代权力关系：公开的暴力和胁迫已被现代权力运行模式所取代，而这一模式依赖于对公民情况的详尽掌控，并通过长期干预来校正公民的行为。正如福柯自己所言："现在要考虑的不是如何用拳头来震慑，而是如何每时每刻全方位约束个体，从而改造制造麻烦的个体。"[1] 福柯认为，这种从肉体惩罚到监视、测评和行为矫正的转向标志着现代性 * 的发端，即我们如今身处的历史阶段。

语言表述

福柯仔细考察了社会上被视作理所应当的某些方面，表述的观点冗长且复杂。在学界，他以繁复艰深的写作风格著称，他的思想即使翻译成英语也晦涩难解。

这种理解上的难度部分缘于福柯有意在写作中试图跳出现有的条条框框。哲学家写作时一般都遵循特定的传统，或是在特定框架下构架观点；而福柯在其作品的开端就构建了一种全新的方法论，并拒绝被归入某一特定的思想流派。社会学家大卫·加兰德等学者指出，"他表述观点所采用的文艺语体和修辞方式，以及他文章中充斥的陌生的术语和概念"使得《规训与惩罚》在学界"恶名远播"，学者们抨击此书言语含混、艰涩难懂。[2]

不过，正是这种恶名激起了学术界围绕其著作展开争论。他在著作中所采用的许多词汇后来都被哲学家、历史学家、社会学家和文化理论家所采纳。他提出的一些概念，如"权力—知识""治理术"*和"凝视"[3]等，经常被用于围绕权力关系的讨论中。

---

1. 大卫·加兰德："福柯的《规训与惩罚》——阐述与评论"，《法律和社会探究》第 11 卷，1986 年第 4 期，第 851 页。
2. 加兰德："福柯的《规训与惩罚》"，第 847 页。
3. 米歇尔·福柯：《规训与惩罚：监狱的诞生》，纽约州谢里登：温特吉出版社，1979 年，第 96 页。

6 思想支脉

要点 🗝

- 福柯认为，家庭、学校和办公室等现代社会结构的运作模式与现代监狱采用的规训手法如出一辙，其核心都是由罪犯或市民将规则内化而实现自我管理。

- 现代社会于福柯而言是一个"监狱连续体"*，在这个连续体中政府迫使民众自我规约。这种观点影响了围绕教育和监狱改革的讨论。

- 福柯在《规训与惩罚》中关于"灵魂"的观点被人们忽略，未能得到充分解读。

其他思想

米歇尔·福柯的《规训与惩罚：监狱的诞生》一书可以被视作对家庭的社会组织的解读，也可以被视作对现代教育系统运作的描写，还能被视作对自我管理的评述。福柯向我们展示了中学、高校、家庭和工作场所等社会机构如何逐渐采用监狱式规训手法来实施管理。

自我约束的观点在福柯后期有关"治理术"的著作中举足轻重。"治理术"指的是让个体遵守某种行为规范的管理方法（即"对行为的管理"）。[1] 换言之，就是政府培养遵规守纪的"理想"公民的方法。后来，福柯在他法兰西公学院的讲演（收录在《安全、领土与人口》[2] 中）及论文"治理术"（发表在《福柯效应：治理术研究》[3]）等文本中都阐述了"治理术"这一重要概念。

尽管不如全景敞视主义的分析透彻（该观点认为，罪犯或普通公民，倘若知道自己正在被监视，便能够自觉地循规蹈矩），福柯对"治理术"概念及其对现代监狱管理方法与其他社会机构相通之处进行的深入研究，有力地推动了围绕权力关系的研究（即如何在社会各部门间分配和行使权力）。

> "须谨记，权力并非一系列否定机制、拒绝机制和排斥机制的集合。相反，权力能进行有效生产。权力生产很有可能直接作用于个体。"
>
> —— 米歇尔·福柯，载《米歇尔·福柯，对话录》

思想探究

众所周知，福柯关注的是对监狱类 * 机构（包括监狱）和自我管理两者间关系的解读。他认为："当个体被置于可见（被监视的）环境中，并且知晓自身身处此境时，个体同时也就承担起权力制约的责任；由此，个体自发地受制于权力，并因为同时承担监视者和被监视者的双重角色而使得自身成为权力关系的一部分；个体成为制约自己的本原。"[4]

对现代监狱演变史的研究和对监视罪犯行为的效应分析使福柯开始思考，其他现代机构如何依赖自我管理。现代社会的运作很大程度上依赖于公民的自我管理，即像被人监视那般循规蹈矩地生活。在这个意义上，政府不仅包括正式的国家结构，还涵盖"自我管理的问题、引导家庭和孩童、管理户籍和指引灵魂等事务"。[5]

"政府"以训练或迫使公民自我管理为基础，通过行使"去中心化"的权力进行统治。香烟盒上"吸烟危害健康"的警示语就是

"治理术"的一个案例。香烟没有被禁，政府也没有惩罚吸烟的人。但是警示语之类的管理措施会促使个体在潜移默化中形成行为规范，使得个体养成某种特定的行为方式。这一规训系统取决于"训示"个体进行自我管理。福柯使用此概念描述先进的自由民主政体（多数西方民主国家以此立国），并认为在这些系统中，学校和医院等机构有着强大的规训作用。[6]这一观点影响了当代围绕教育、监狱改革和公共政策而展开的争论。

福柯著作中另一重要的分论题考察身体和个体是通过什么方式被统治的，他将这一过程命名为"行为控制"。[7]例如，监狱或少管所制定严格的规训式作息时间表，使得身体完全受制于时间层面上的规训，通过每时每刻密不透风的安排，牢牢控制住身体。伴随时刻表而来的则是体能机制的转变。监视和规训机制界定了身体和其对象之间的关系。此种情况不仅见于监狱或少管所，还有现代办公场所，在这里，个体可能会担心因为自己午餐花费时间较长、早退或在办公室做了与工作无关的事而招致经理或同事的白眼。考虑到经理可能会撞见自己早退，员工往往选择自我约束而不早退。

福柯用这些例子来论证，"监狱连续体"[8]事实上涵盖了社会组织机构的整体模式。该连续体的特征是注重辨别异常（即不恰当或违反规则的行为）和关注反常。此外，这一框架对微不足道的逾越和滔天大罪等量齐观，将相同的规训机制施加于所有个体身上。

被忽视之处

这部著作有一个方面尚未被深入研究，即福柯对于"灵魂"的理解。尽管福柯本人声称《规训与惩罚》一书的目的在于"从谱系学立场考虑现代灵魂"，[9]但从字里行间来看，他关注的仍是塑造灵魂的权力网，而非灵魂本身。

福柯所说的"灵魂"即犹太—基督教传统中的灵魂。这一概念与福柯其他有关知识和权力的论述密切相关，因为灵魂取代身体，成为刑罚改革和监视的重点对象。福柯之所以如此重视灵魂，是因为现代规训过程构建并创造了灵魂。没有规训、监视和人类科学〔包括以监管和检查机制为核心的犯罪学*（犯罪学是研究犯罪和犯罪行为的学科）、心理学*以及精神病学〕的存在，诸如此类合乎规范的灵魂便不复存在。

福柯写道："这个真实的、非肉体的灵魂并不是一种物质层面上的存在；它体现某种权力效应，并指涉某种知识形式。"[10]传统的犹太—基督教认为身体是禁锢灵魂的狱所，福柯却反驳称灵魂才是"身体的狱所"。[11]

其他学者也引用过这一概念来探讨现代身份认同。例如，著名社会理论家尼古拉斯·罗斯*就将此作为《管理灵魂》一书的理论基石。全书首先梳理了20世纪心理学实践方面的一些重要观点，接着试图通过分析法将心理学延伸到经济生活中，这一尝试与福柯的做法如出一辙：即考察社会学专家如何塑造了我们的生活和自我认知。他们著书立说，试图将政府管理的政治和社会目标与个体欲望、愉悦和情感联结起来；这一尝试是通过自我实现来达成制度目标。[12]

1. 格雷厄姆·布希尔等编：《福柯效应：治理术研究》，伊利诺伊州芝加哥：芝加哥大学出版社，1991年，第2页。

2. 米歇尔·福柯：《安全、领土与人口：1977—1978年在法兰西公学院的讲演》，伦敦和纽约：帕尔格雷夫·麦克米伦出版社，2007年。

3. 布希尔等编：《福柯效应》。

4. 米歇尔·福柯：《规训与惩罚：监狱的诞生》，纽约州谢里登：温特吉出版社，1979年，第202—203页。

5. 托马斯·莱姆基："'生命政治学的诞生'：米歇尔·福柯在法兰西公学院关于新自由主义治理术的讲演"，《经济与社会》第30卷，2001年第2期，第2页。

6. 米歇尔·福柯："治理术"，《福柯精选》，保罗·雷恩博和尼古拉斯·罗斯编，纽约和伦敦：新新出版社，2003年，第102—103页。

7. 福柯：《规训与惩罚》，第149页。

8. 福柯：《规训与惩罚》，第293页。

9. 福柯：《规训与惩罚》，第23页。

10. 福柯：《规训与惩罚》，第29页。

11. 福柯，《规训与惩罚》，第29页。

12. 尼古拉斯·罗斯：《管理灵魂：个体自我的形塑》，肯塔基州佛罗伦萨：泰勒与弗朗西斯出版集团／劳特利奇出版社，1990年，第258页。

7 历史成就

要点 🗝

- 米歇尔·福柯的《规训与惩罚》从根本上重新界定了社会学家和哲学家对于现代权力关系的理解方式，以及此种权力关系在塑造社会、文化和个体身份中所扮演的角色。

- 当时社会政治环境，即20世纪六七十年代法国社会掀起的激进政治运动，影响了人们对这部著作的反应，当然该著作对此也有所反映。

- 尽管《规训与惩罚》一书的反响不错，但并非没有批评之声。例如，社会学家齐格蒙特·鲍曼*就认为，如今，大多数人并非被胁迫，而是受到诱惑才去遵守社会规范。

观点评价

　　米歇尔·福柯的《规训与惩罚》通过回顾现代刑罚体系的发展史，试图阐明现代机构的权力演变史。他追溯了现代监狱的演化史，说明了对罪犯的惩罚从最初的公开行刑转变为以监视和控制为主的行为矫正，由此阐明了权力、知识、个体和顺从之间的关系。古代或封建刑罚制度和现代刑罚制度的主要区别在于，后者的重点是改造罪犯。通过监视和控制，这一刑罚体系得以按照自己的偏好改造个体，以确保个体遵从特定的举止规范。通过收集有关其改造对象的知识，这一体系得以深入了解其对象的行为及行为背后的动机，进而制定规则，促使个体自我约束。

　　福柯展示了这一全新权力形式的深远影响。监视和知识收集是现代监狱的运行原则，而学校、医院、工厂和办公室等机构的运作方式与此并无二致。此外，社会科学领域惯用的数据收集、对象监控和状态诊断等研究方法都依循同样原理：科学和人文领域学术思想的推进也归功于现代规训机制的运作原则。

> "本书旨在讲述现代灵魂与一种新的审判权力之间的关系演变史。"
>
> —— 米歇尔·福柯：《规训与惩罚：监狱的诞生》

当时的成就

福柯的作品从根本上重新界定了哲学和社会学领域，深刻影响了刑罚社会学*——它是社会学的分支，主要研究刑罚和社会之间的关系。在《规训与惩罚》出版之前，这一社会学分支主要基于埃米尔·杜尔凯姆*的思想。[1]杜尔凯姆是 19 世纪末 20 世纪初社会学发展的学科奠基人，强调社会机构和社会结构在社会生活管理中所发挥的作用。在 20 世纪 70 年代之前，关于刑罚的研究基本都由犯罪学家（研究犯罪行为和罪犯的学者）和刑罚学家*（研究刑罚和监狱的学者）承担，他们将刑罚视作技术问题，而非社会学问题。换言之，他们的目的是研究如何让刑罚更加有效，而并不关注社会机构刑罚执行方式的演变历史及影响。

从这个意义上来说，福柯的著作不仅拓宽了他自身所从事领域中的知识视野，还为理解众多学科领域中的权力关系开辟了新路径。

抛开著作本身做出的主要贡献，当时的社会政治形势也明显影响了人们对该书的评论。20 世纪 60 年代末及 70 年代初，法国社会掀起诸多激进社会运动，包括 1968 年巴黎的五月风暴、民众对法国介入越南战争的声讨以及法国知识分子群体中酝酿的反殖民情绪——这些都使得福柯的思想在彼时与读者产生共鸣。知识分子对当时法国的教育体制、充斥着精英主义的学术风气以及当局对殖民地的压迫十分不满，而福柯正当其时地提出，顺从正是在权力和知识的双重作用下产生的，这一观点在当时自然而然地吸引了一大批读者。

局限性

《规训与惩罚》于 1975 年首次出版，该书讨论了诸多当时的社会政治问题，常常被视为一部反映 20 世纪六七十年代法国左翼思想的作品。然而，该书之所以成为人文社科领域的重要著作，不仅因为书中传达的思想超前，还因为该书虽然属于社会学、哲学和历史学著作，但并不局限于这些领域。福柯梳理了从中世纪到现代性发端时期（现代时期）惩罚形式的演变史，并发现了现代规训的雏形，这一史学研究方法被专门用来理解不同历史时期、不同情境中的权力形式。

在书中，福柯关注的并非 20 世纪六七十年代法国的权力机制，而是抽象层面的现代权力的运作，即权力在任一现代情境中如何运作。他的核心观点是监视、控制和知识采集的作用，而他的这些观点适用于各种情境设定，并不局限于特定的治理形式。因此，即便是对于生活在 21 世纪新自由主义 * 的全球化 * 经济体之下的读者而言，福柯的思想仍不失其意义，因为这一体系的运作同样依赖监控机制、数据收集和对公民的监视。（此处"新自由主义"指当下的正统经济学模式，即认为经济增长的动力源自不受监管的自由贸易、私有化和尽可能少的政府干预等；"全球化"指全球范围内经济和文化加速融合的趋势。）事实上，考虑到当下的科技发展，包括互联网和闭路电视的诞生——这些都是福柯时代所没有的，我们甚至可以说与其刚出版时相比，《规训与惩罚》一书中的思想在当下更具现实意义。这也解释了为何现代研究数字文化*的学者时常会借鉴该书的观点。

尽管《规训与惩罚》产生了积极的影响，但并非没有批评之声。例如，著名社会学家齐格蒙特·鲍曼就认为，规训式社会的出现标志着现代性的发展已步入特定阶段，这一时期各个阶层的人口数量庞大，需要进行有效管理。这是一个军队化和工业化的时代。然而，按照福柯的构想，规训式社会的重要性在后现代时期会逐渐减弱。而在鲍曼看来："大部分人……选择成为社会群体的一部分，是出于被引诱而非被管辖，是出于广告宣传的效果而非教化使然，是出于需求而非服从规则。"[2]换言之，我们之所以成为某类主体，是受到引诱，而非监控所致。例如，我们希望成为身材匀称、健康的个体，这并非由于我们正处在权威的监视之中，而是因为广告宣传诱导我们想要变得身材匀称、身体健康。

---

1. 见埃米尔·杜尔凯姆和路易斯·A.柯塞：《社会分工论》，纽约州纽约：自由出版社，1997年。
2. 齐格蒙特·鲍曼："论性的后现代运用"，《理论、文化与社会》第15卷，1998年第3期，第23页。

8 著作地位

要点 ⚷

- 终其一生，米歇尔·福柯都在探讨历史、常态和非常态之间的关系。他尤其关注社会机构如何给越界的人贴上标签来强制执行某种特定行为准则。

- 《规训与惩罚》属于福柯最后出版的几本著作之一，学者们将此书视作福柯"谱系学"研究的开端，并将其与福柯早期的"考古学"*研究区分开来。

- 从福利国家*（该体制下政府为其公民提供一定的保障）到新自由主义国家（该体制下政府尽可能不干涉公民的经济生活），国家和公民之间的关系不断变迁，但该部著作对于理解国家与公民之间的关系一直非常重要。

定位

米歇尔·福柯长期关注"疯癫"或"犯罪"这类标签在创建和维持权力结构以及向公民灌输行为规范中所发挥的作用，《规训与惩罚：监狱的诞生》正是这一思考的产物。譬如，在《疯癫与文明》（1961）一书中，福柯将精神病与"疯癫"作了区分。他强调，后者是一种社会建构，被机构用来标记不循规蹈矩的个体。与其后期著作一样，福柯在《疯癫与文明》一书中采用历史研究法，通过考察医学史，来批判有关精神健康和所谓"正常人"的现代臆断。

福柯的后期著作，包括《临床医学的诞生》（1963）和《词与物》（1966），对上述的一些思想做了延伸。18 世纪末到 19 世纪初正是社会变革、新技术突飞猛进的时期，福柯在《临床医学的诞生》中便梳理了这一时期的医学史。《词与物》对科学进行整体考察，认为纵观历史，科学话语不得不将某些假设视为"真理"，然而这些所谓的事实在每个时代却不尽相同。

福柯于 20 世纪 60 年代后期开始撰写《规训与惩罚》，这是他学术生涯后期的代表作。然而福柯却常常说它是自己的"第一本书"[1]，因为他认为自己的思想在此书中已发展成熟，并得到了最忠实的阐述。该书也是理解福柯后期思想的一座桥梁；比方说，在《规训与惩罚》中福柯首次提到"治理术"，他在后续著作中也对此概念作了进一步深化。

> "如果你的举止异于他人，那你就不正常；既然你不正常，那么你就生病了。事实上，这三个范畴——异于他人、不正常和生病——完全不是一回事，但社会常常将这三者等同起来。"
>
> ——米歇尔·福柯，载《米歇尔·福柯，对话录》

整合

福柯穷其一生都在考察历史、权力—知识，常态化*和自我管理等概念。《规训与惩罚》虽然探讨了上述概念，但同时也偏离了他此前作品所采用的研究路径。福柯在该书中首次采用"谱系学"方法从事史学研究，而非他之前发表的历史学论著中所采用的"知识考古学"方法。这两种史学研究方法在许多重要的方面都有所不同。

考古学方法的理论基础是：思想体系受到个体潜意识机制的规

约。这一方法将知识体系与其产生条件放在一起加以考察。因此，可以将这一研究过程视为探索可能性的过程：即探寻形成思想的潜在性因素的生成过程。不同于现象学和传统史学的哲学研究方法，考古学方法并未借用个体心理学的表达方式，而是关注思想、观念和话语实践＊（即影响知识产生的特定文化和历史因素）的形成。因此，考古学只能对比不同历史时期或不同情境下的话语实践和认知方式，而并不能解释思想变迁的**缘由**，或是话语实践中的变动。

福柯的谱系学概念意在弥补这一理论和方法上的缺失。此概念援引了弗里德里希·尼采所提出的"道德的谱系"概念。《规训与惩罚》一书采用谱系学方法，旨在说明任一给定的知识体系或思想体系的出现都是突发历史事件的产物，是在此之前的历史演变的结果。换言之，谱系学研究将当下和过去连接起来，追溯过去以解释当下。福柯的谱系学方法关注特定学科或信仰体系的形成机制——也就是说，众所周知的"真理"是如何被创造的。福柯将这个过程及其内在运作机制称为"话语制度的权术"。[2] 福柯终其一生都在挑战哲学话语本身，并质疑哲学研究的发展趋势，在他看来，这种趋势使得哲学研究失去了批判意识。因此，从广义上来讲，《规训与惩罚》一书发扬了福柯的这一观点。

意义

尽管西方的社会经济形态早已发生变化，但福柯的《规训与惩罚》仍具有现实意义，甚至比福柯当初预期的还要有价值。20世纪60年代至70年代，福柯伏案著书，而这一时期，布雷顿森林体系＊被废除，与此同时，金融哲学——福利国家体制的理论基石——也土崩瓦解。

布雷顿森林体系是第二次世界大战结束以后至 20 世纪 70 年代初期全球范围内实行的一种货币管理体制，用于调节主要工业经济体间的商业和金融关系。与当今体制相比，该体系下的政府在国际、国内权力关系运作中扮演着更为重要的角色。在"福利国家"中，国有机构和国家项目为公民提供各类服务——包括医疗、社会保障和其他社会福利。

在这两种体制下，福柯所描述的动态关系发生在政府官员和公民之间：例如社工和青少年罪犯之间，心理医生和病人之间，或假释官和其假释对象之间。福柯主要关注的是这些国家机器所采用的规训机制。福柯批判的潜台词是：社会福利工作和医疗等向来被我们认为是进步的、非政治化的和慈善的特殊行业，事实上却是压迫 *、监视和控制公民的规训机构。

福柯的思想在新自由主义体制下同样适用性很广，新自由主义是取代布雷顿森林体系且延续至今的经济体制。新自由主义的一系列经济政策倡导经济自由化、自由贸易、开放市场、私有化、解除管制和强化私有经济；然而，和它所取代的经济体制一样，新自由主义体制同样带来了关乎监视、个人隐私和选择权的困扰。[3] 从这个意义上说，《规训与惩罚》一书的价值从未消退，在当下全球化的世界中，该书所探讨的问题与学者和批评家们的担忧仍旧息息相关。

该书之所以影响深远，就在于它的永恒性和普适性。书中对于权力、知识、监视和个体间关系的考察，影响了当今数字时代下关于隐私、数据搜集和信息传播及使用的讨论。《规训与惩罚》重新界定了社会学和哲学领域，是理解当今社会权力关系的重要文献。

1. 詹姆斯·米勒:《福柯的生死爱欲》, 马萨诸塞州坎布里奇: 哈佛大学出版社, 1993 年。

2. 米歇尔·福柯:《权力 / 知识: 谈话录及其他作品选集, 1972—1977》, 纽约: 兰登书屋数字出版社, 1980 年, 第 118 页。

3. 南希·弗雷泽: "从规训到灵活化? 在全球化背景下重读福柯",《星座》第 10 卷, 2003 年第 2 期, 第 160—171 页。

第三部分：学术影响

9 最初反响

要点 🔑—

- 米歇尔·福柯的《规训与惩罚》在出版后便招致批评，其中最著名的批判主要来自社会科学家、哲学家尤尔根·哈贝马斯。福柯对启蒙时代（欧洲思想史的特定阶段）思想的批判以及他认为理性是由社会建构的这一观点颇为哈贝马斯所诟病。

- 在福柯的晚年，他和哈贝马斯因这些议题发生了争论。

- 《规训与惩罚》也曾因未能精确描述监狱内部的权力运作而受到批判。

批评

米歇尔·福柯的《规训与惩罚》一经出版就遭受了猛烈的批评。其中最为人所知的批评来自德高望重的社会科学家兼哲学家尤尔根·哈贝马斯。哈贝马斯的指责以及随后所引发的学界著名的"福柯与哈贝马斯之争"持续了数年，争论内容涵盖了双方的诸多著作。

哈贝马斯是当代对启蒙时代的理性信念最为坚定的捍卫者，他从一个完全不同的视角，即从他称之为"交际理性"*和"话语伦理学"的维度来理解权力。[1] 他想借此表达，理性是可能的，理性是成功沟通的结果。福柯并不认同固定人物性格的存在，他认为理性是历史形成的，是偶然性的产物（也就是强调历史语境的重要性）；而哈贝马斯则反驳称存在固定的人物性格，并且理性可以使人类脱离困境。

其次，哈贝马斯认为，只有促进自由交流的行为才能推动合法社会组织的产生。这一理论的整体观点与福柯的思想截然相反，因为福柯认为社会交往本身总是被权力所构建和限制。此外，他还认为福柯错误地将所有文化和政治运动归类为暴力行为，将社会生活简单归纳为一系列的权力制约。

哈贝马斯和福柯的研究方法也互相冲突。哈贝马斯指责福柯是"完全反社会学的"，声称福柯没有遵循科学的研究方法。[2]其他批评者，如政治哲学家南希·弗雷泽*也曾因相似原因批评福柯的研究；弗雷泽认为，福柯在鼓励我们批评现代社会的同时，又一直向我们灌输这种批判是没有意义的，因为我们无法摆脱权力的控制。

> "不断地进行划分，直到把所有人都划分为正常人和非正常人，这是把以往对付麻风病人的非此即彼、打上标记、予以放逐的方法应用到当下完全不同的对象上。由于有了一系列完整的衡量、监视和矫正非正常人的技术和制度，过去因恐惧瘟疫而诞生的规训机制得以启用。"
>
> ——米歇尔·福柯:《规训与惩罚：监狱的诞生》

回应

福柯对哈贝马斯最著名的回应之一在其晚年所写的文章《什么是启蒙？》之中。在此文中，福柯称现代性和启蒙是一种态度而非历史的某一阶段。研究现代性和启蒙，目的不在于发现人类的普世价值或特征，而在于理解人类的起源和发展。另外，我们应当考虑的是成为哪一种自我，而不是去追寻基本人性。

福柯坚称自己对真理和权力的看法比哈贝马斯认为的有着更

多的细微差别。他将自己的研究视为对比理性和非理性的实践性研究，而不是对理性的可能性批判。对于福柯而言，他的整个研究都在试图证明社会对理性和非理性的界定——以及对于它们在层级制度中的定位——都过于简单化。

福柯也驳斥了哈贝马斯认为真理和理性是绝对的（指事物非对即错）这一观点。哈贝马斯认为理性就是真理。真理只有一个，而真理和非真理之间存在明确的区别。但是福柯认为这种二分法是一种"知识胁迫"。[3] 他认为，理性具有很强的主观性：它是一种社会性的构建（即特定社会环境的产物），依赖于历史和文化情境。对于福柯来说，"理性是自主产生的，这也就是我为什么尝试分析理性的形式：理性在不同的基础、不同的创造过程、不同的变动之中相克相生"。[4] 福柯认为，我们如何设想特定事情为真的过程才是值得研究的：福柯对于特定知识体系的形成，以及它们如何破坏或肯定现存的权力机制兴趣浓厚。对知识本身的批判——包括我们对真理的理解和我们的反思过程——是他研究的重点之一。

冲突与共识

在该书出版 40 年后，围绕《规训与惩罚》的辩论仍未停止。例如，政治心理学家 C. 弗雷德·阿尔福德 * 批判福柯的方法论，并称之为方法论错误。[5] 阿尔福德基于自己在美国从事监狱人类学研究的经历，称规训行为——即福柯的立论基础——事实上在现代监狱中并不存在，并提出了对立原则倒是显而易见的。阿尔福德认为，监狱的惩戒是通过对出入的控制而非持续监管的可能性来实现的——对出入的控制使得监管变得无用。他认为监狱当局并不看管犯人，因为他们的权力已经体现在可以直接出入监狱方面。他们有不加看管的权力。阿尔福德称，福柯有关监狱的理论和观点不符合历史事实。比如，福柯的理论中提到"全景式监狱"，这里面的囚犯永远不能确定他们是否正在被监视，这种监狱在现实中并不存在，然而福柯却在其著述中假设此种监狱改革已经开始，由此他误把理论概念当作实践操作，而这进一步混淆了他对权力的理解。

　　如果说以上对福柯著述的批评在学界早有先声，阿尔福德还进一步批判福柯，指出他在创作中想当然地认为，新的规训做法不同于过去的或更为"传统的"权力运作模式。阿尔福德驳斥福柯的观点，认为规训措施实际上是由所有统治者和权威机构施行的。

---

1. 尤尔根·哈贝马斯：《交往行为理论（第1卷）：行为合理性与社会合理化》，马萨诸塞州波士顿：灯塔出版社，1984年。
2. 迪迪埃·埃里蓬：《米歇尔·福柯及其同时代人》，巴黎：法雅出版社，1994年，第155—186页。
3. 米歇尔·福柯："什么是启蒙？"，载《福柯效应：治理术研究》，格雷厄姆·布希尔等编，伊利诺伊州芝加哥：芝加哥大学出版社，1991年，第42页。
4. 转引自迈克尔·凯利等：《批判与权力：重铸福柯和哈贝马斯之争》，马萨诸塞州坎布里奇；伦敦：麻省理工学院出版社，1994年，第119页。
5. C.费雷德·阿尔福德："如果福柯关于监狱的所言都是错误的会怎样？《规训与惩罚》问世二十年后"，《理论和社会》第29卷，2000年第1期，第125—146页。

10 后续争议

要点 ⚷━━

- 尽管《规训与惩罚》一书的基本假设招致猛烈批评，诸多学科领域中的学者仍接受了书中的观点。

- 该书推动了社会学领域关于惩罚的研究（分析施行惩罚的原因与方式），同时也有助于社会学诸多分支中的术语形成，其中包括组织社会学*（社会学的一个分支，研究社会组织）和法律社会学*。

- 学者们发现诸如"权力—知识"和"规训"之类的概念非常有用。

应用与问题

米歇尔·福柯的《规训与惩罚》如今依然是社会学家、哲学家、理论家、社会科学家以及人文学科的学者们从事研究所需的重要文本。紧跟福柯脚步的新生派作家们运用《规训与惩罚》中的概念，例如规训和全景敞视主义，来观照权力和现代个体的交叠。学者们以福柯的理论洞见为框架，考察福柯从未预见过的一系列问题，例如肥胖症[1]或是人力资源管理[*2]。

即便如此，《规训与惩罚》还是遭人诟病。在该书出版后的几年里，福柯所做的讲演被收录于《安全、领土与人口》一书中。在这些讲演中，他批判了自身早年研究中的某些观点，认为自己当时过度关注规训对于个体自由的限制。福柯完善了早期的观点，称我们必须将权力视为一种关心"人的自由、人们想做什么、人们有兴趣做什么以及人们考虑做什么"的机制和"一项依赖于每个人的自由才能实行的规则"。³ 社会理论家尼古拉斯·罗斯在《自由的权力：重构政治思想》⁴ 一书中对此观点做了延伸，用以研究现代治理如何管理个人自由。

其他一些学者试图更新福柯对全景敞视主义的界定。例如，挪威社会学家托马斯·马蒂森称，权力存在于他所称之的"共景监狱"（在共景监狱里，多数人看管少数人），而非全景式监狱（全景式监狱中少数人看管多数人）。马蒂森指出，我们生活在一个观察者社会而非规训式社会。他以名人文化的兴起以及大众媒体为例，指出代表大众的"多数人"通过观察"少数人"的行为来指导自身的行为，这些"少数人"指的是当今文化中的名人、政客或其他公众人物。⁵

> "人体正在进入一种探究它、打碎它和重新编排它的权力机制。一种'政治解剖学'，或者说一种'权力力学'正在冉冉升起。它规定了人们如何通过所选择的技术，按照预定的速度和效果来控制其他人的肉体，使后者不仅'做什么'，而且'怎么做'都符合前者的愿望。这样，规训就能制造出一批驯服的、训练有素的肉体，即'驯顺的'肉体。"
>
> —— 米歇尔·福柯：《规训与惩罚：监狱的诞生》

思想流派

从 20 世纪 70 年代末开始，出现了研究监狱类机构（即监禁人的场所）的新范式，这类研究大多关注监狱在建立和维持社会秩序方面的作用，而非惩罚本身。这些新研究可以被统称为惩罚社会学，该分支以福柯著作中的概念为基石，其中包括国家控制以及个体成为社会主体的过程。

福柯的研究在许多方面推动了新研究的发展。首先，据一位学者所言，福柯"向众多历史学家和社会理论家们呈现了惩罚在社会学上的深远影响，以及通过细致考察惩罚行为所能获得的洞见"。[6]福柯的作品还为理解国家控制提供了理论工具。惩罚社会学这一分支学科沿用了福柯有关刑罚和罪犯管理的观点，并对其加以完善。这些变化极为重要，并且体现在社会学家讨论法律、刑罚、控制和国家权力的用语中："规训""监视""权力—知识"和"常规化"等都成为当代社会学词汇中的常用术语。

法律社会学家们也纷纷效仿，[7]试图构建理论框架，在这一框架下法律被视作管理和规训机制；一些学者甚至构想出"福柯式法学理论"，强调用各种方式将法律理解为一种治理形式。

当代研究

《规训与惩罚》在整个社会科学和人文科学领域广为流传。近年来，与之联系并不紧密的社会学分支——组织社会学和管理学吸收了该书的某些重要理念以及福柯研究的主体思想，罕见地将其运用到社会科学和社会生活的其他领域。例如，美国社会地理学家兼食品专家朱莉·古斯曼使用"权力—知识"概念来探讨健康理念和食物获取渠道两者之间如何互动，进而造成社会群体之间显著的不平等现象。[8]同时，英国管理经济学家芭芭拉·汤利*认为人力资源管理行为最应当被视为一种话语体制，这种管理机制采用类似于全景式监狱的主体塑造手法，[9]使得员工易于管理。同样的，组织理论家吉布森·伯雷尔的著作研究了机构如何成为监视和规训机制。[10]

52

特别是对于组织社会学和行政科学这两个学科而言，《规训与惩罚》一书仍做出了极富原创性的贡献。组织社会学在很大程度上依赖理性和效率这类概念，并且极大地（虽然经常是以令人不适的方式）受惠于福柯式分析，即探讨权力、治理的本质，以及牵涉其中的个体。

---

1. 朱莉·古斯曼和梅勒妮·迪普伊："新自由主义的表征：经济、文化和肥胖之权术"，《环境和规划D：社会和空间》第24卷，2006年第3期，第427—448页。
2. 芭芭拉·汤利："福柯，权力/知识，及其与人力资源管理的相关性"，《管理评论学刊》第18卷，1993年第3期，第518—545页。
3. 米歇尔·福柯：《安全、领土与人口：1977—1978在法兰西公学院的讲演》，伦敦和纽约：帕尔格雷夫·麦克米伦出版社，2007年，第49页。
4. 尼古拉斯·罗斯：《自由的权力：重构政治思想》，剑桥：剑桥大学出版社，1999年。
5. 托马斯·马蒂森："观察者社会：重溯福柯的全景式监狱"，《犯罪学理论》第1卷，1997年第2期。
6. 大卫·加兰德："社会学中惩罚的探讨框架"，《英国社会学杂志》第41卷，1990年第1期，第2页。
7. 参见艾伦·亨特和盖里·威克姆：《福柯与法律：作为管理的法律社会学》，科罗拉多州波德；伦敦：普鲁托出版社，1994年。
8. 古斯曼和迪普伊："新自由主义的表征"，第427—448页。
9. 汤利："福柯，权力/知识"，第518—545页。
10. 吉布森·布瑞尔："现代主义、后现代主义和组织分析2：米歇尔·福柯的贡献"，《组织研究》第9卷，1988年第2期，第221—235页。

11 当代印迹

要点 🔑

- 米歇尔·福柯的《规训与惩罚》在其所属的社会学及史学领域都被视为核心作品，在其他人文学科以及社会科学领域中也是如此。

- 福柯的观点被用于考察诸多议题，包括肥胖、性、伦理以及认识论视角下的国家地位——即根据理论，我们对国家能够认知到的部分以及认识的方式。

- 由于学者们对理性的看法各不相同，探讨还在持续，福柯与哈贝马斯之争甚至在福柯去世后仍在进行。

地位

米歇尔·福柯的《规训与惩罚》依然是诸多领域的核心文本，特别是在历史、人类学和社会学领域。虽然并非亦步亦趋，但是社会学家们沿袭了福柯对权力、话语（在福柯看来，话语指历史和权力双重作用下产生的言说方式；不过此术语一般是指通过交流想法来定义如何理解某事物）、身体和个体建构的关注。这些都是福柯在其著作中细致考察的主题。

组织社会学家南希·弗雷泽、[1] 政治社会学家芭芭拉·汤利以及社会发展学者詹姆斯·弗格森[2] 都在他们的作品中使用了"话语"这一概念。特别是南希·弗雷泽，她的言论颇为偏激——她指出，福柯有关规训的学说虽然创作于20世纪五六十年代（政府干预和对福利国家制度的支持与投资是当时正统经济模式的两大特点），但仍适用于当今全球化下的新自由主义国家，在这些国家里市场自行发展，而并不优先考虑社会正义和福利。弗雷泽研究了福柯有关国家和市场如何围绕自我管理来创造话语的观点。同样，如大卫·加兰德、[3] 约阿希姆·斯维德贝格 [4] 和约翰·布雷斯韦特 [5] 等惩罚和犯罪社会学家都受到福柯将惩罚视为一种社会控制形式这一观点的影响。

　　一些学者吸收了福柯研究中关于人类身体的观点，并将其应用于他们重点研究的多种理论性议题上，如肥胖症、[6] 女性主义研究、[7] 酷儿理论 [*8]（研究性别和身份，该理论的基本观点往往颠覆了对性别和身份的传统理解）以及解剖学 [9] 的发展。福柯将身体视为规训的场所和规训技术的目标对象；这些思想家们受此观点启发，得以理解少数派或是边缘群体如何被迫顺从。

　　同时，国家理论学家罗伯特·杰索普 [10] 和托马斯·莱姆基 [11] 借鉴福柯的思想来分析政府，包括"权力—知识" [12] 的向心性和国家内部的话语实践（即知识的生产和管理）。在杰索普和莱姆基看来，福柯的学说是理解国家治理技术的基础。他们认为，福柯改变了我们对国家的看法，我们不再视国家为自上而下实行统治的单一实体，而是将国家治理视为众多行为者之行为和实践的集成。关于这一看法的改变，例证之一就是政府与非营利组织或慈善团体之间的合作，这些组织会向药物滥用者及其他做出越轨行为的人们提供援救。这些做法大多基于规训机制，即通过个体的自我管理来实现。

> "对于工厂、学校、兵营和医院与监狱如出一辙，这一现象难道值得大惊小怪吗？"
>
> ——米歇尔·福柯：《规训与惩罚：监狱的诞生》

互动

《规训与惩罚》一书涉及历史学、社会学、犯罪学知识和文化理论，可以说它属于这些学科领域，也可以说它不仅仅属于这些学科中的任何一个，所以很难将其归类为任何一个子学科或是已有传统学科。因此，福柯的理论对当今思想家影响深远，这也是为什么诸多学科领域都解读了这部作品。例如，人类学家詹姆斯·法比昂在其伦理学的研究中运用了福柯有关社会机构的思想；[13]古典学者大卫·拉莫尔曾在其有关性与古代的研究中引用了福柯的作品；[14]历史学家瓦兹拉·柴明达尔曾在关于边界和市民的论述中采纳了福柯作品中提出的有关个体身份塑造和规训的观点。[15]

这些迥然不同的福柯派学者们的共同之处在于：他们都倾向于追溯机构的历史演变、辨识社会控制和沿用福柯式谱系学研究路径。福柯的方法论适用范围广泛，为这些研究带来了极大帮助，借助此种方法，学者们可以考察知识和权力在任何领域或是历史语境下的传播。

持续争议

福柯于 1984 年逝世之时，他和社会学家尤尔根·哈贝马斯的积怨刚散，这一积怨源于他们之间持续数年的论战。因此福柯的追随者们延续了这一辩论。此辩论围绕理性的本质展开，引申开来也就是人类解放*（即从奴役状态中解放）的可能性。研究理性和批判理论的学者们积极参与了此场延续福柯与哈贝马斯之争的论战，论战涉及社会理论的一种基本原则：人类社会是否在本质上就容易产生冲突。

哈贝马斯批判福柯提出的相对主义（即福柯认为，在特定事物中并不存在绝对原则），而福柯的追随者们大多认为这一批判是站不住脚的，因为循此思路，哈贝马斯"预设了试图证明的结论"。[16] 其他人继而指出，哈贝马斯的这一分析基于对福柯作品观点的误读。这些学者里包括迈克尔·凯利，他为福柯辩护，称哈贝马斯误解了福柯有关具有规训效应的权力以及地域批判的学说。凯利认为，虽然福柯批评了自启蒙时代以来一直占据主导地位的理性观念，但他从未断言理性本身是无价值的。[17] 此外，社会学家萨曼莎·艾舍登和大卫·欧文于 1999 年出版了合著《福柯对战哈贝马斯：重铸谱系学和批判理论间的对话》，在此书中，他们就哈贝马斯后期对福柯的批判尝试性地提出"福柯式反驳"，为这场持续已久的论战注入新的活力。

1. 南希·弗雷泽："从规训到灵活化？在全球化背景下重读福柯"，《星座》第 10 卷，2003 年第 2 期。

2. 詹姆斯·弗格森：《反政治机器：索莱托的发展、去政治化和官僚式权力》，明尼阿波利斯：明尼苏达大学出版社，1994 年。

3. 参见大卫·加兰德："社会学中惩罚的探讨框架"，《英国社会学杂志》第 41 卷，1990 年第 1 期。

4. 约阿希姆·J.斯维德贝格："知识、控制和刑事惩罚"，《美国社会学杂志》第 99 卷，1994 年第 4 期，第 911—943 页。

5. 约翰·布雷斯韦特："惩罚社会学怎么了？"，《理论犯罪学》第 7 卷，2003 年第 1 期，第 5—28 页。

6. 朱莉·古斯曼和梅勒妮·迪普伊："新自由主义的表征：经济、文化和肥胖之权术"，《环境和规划 D：社会和空间》第 24 卷，2006 年第 3 期，第 427—448 页。

7. 嘉娜·萨威基:《规训福柯:女性主义、权力和身体》,伦敦:劳特利奇出版社,1991年;苏珊·海克曼编:《米歇尔·福柯作品的女性主义解读》,宾夕法尼亚州宾州大学帕克分校:宾夕法尼亚州立大学出版社,1996年。

8. 大卫·哈波林:《圣人福柯:一部同性恋圣徒传》,牛津和纽约:牛津大学出版社,1997年。

9. 简·C.鲁普:"米歇尔·福柯、身体政治及现代解剖学的兴起与发展",《历史社会学杂志》第5卷,1992年第1期,第31—60页。

10. 鲍勃·杰索普:"从微观权力到治理术:福柯有关国家地位、国家形成、治国之道和国家权力的著述",《政治地理学》第26卷,2007年第1期,第34—40页。

11. 托马斯·莱姆基:"难以消化的一餐?福柯、治理术和国家理论",《Distinktion:斯堪的纳维亚社会理论杂志》第8卷,2007年第2期,第43—64页。

12. 米歇尔·福柯:《规训与惩罚:监狱的诞生》,纽约州谢里登:温特吉出版社,1979年,第27页。

13. 詹姆斯·D.法比昂:"伦理人类学:福柯和自我教育",《代表》第74卷,2001年第1期,第83—104页。

14. 大卫·H.J.拉莫尔等:《对性的再思考:福柯和古典时期》,新泽西州普林斯顿:普林斯顿大学出版社,1997年。

15. 瓦兹拉·法齐拉亚·克巴里·柴明达尔:《长期分裂和现代南亚的形成:难民、边界和历史》,纽约州纽约:哥伦比亚大学出版社,2007年。

16. 萨曼莎·艾舍登和大卫·欧文:《福柯对战哈贝马斯:重铸谱系学和批判理论间的对话》,加利福尼亚州千橡市;伦敦:赛奇出版社,1999年。

17. 迈克尔·凯利等:《批判与权力:重铸福柯和哈贝马斯之争》,马萨诸塞州坎布里奇;伦敦:麻省理工学院出版社,1994年,第372页。

12 未来展望

要点 ⚷

- 在关注现代权力关系的人文和社会学科学者眼中，米歇尔·福柯的《规训与惩罚》仍然是重要的文本。

- 该书被广泛应用到当代对数字监管机制和个人隐私方面的讨论中。它对关于健康和疾病的社会学研究也产生了显著影响。

- 福柯的研究具有永恒意义，因其研究了权力关系中运用的技术和机制，而不是公开攻击某一特定群体或机构的权力行使方式。

潜力

米歇尔·福柯的《规训与惩罚》仍然是人文和社会学科学者们的重要研究文本，而且在社会学领域之外也有广泛运用，包括国际关系、数字文化研究、法律、文学研究、女性主义批评、酷儿理论和文化理论等多个分布极广的领域。这是一个自相矛盾的现象，因为福柯的创作是对学术话语的批判，与后来那些吸纳他观点的领域又是相对立的。

如何将福柯的研究运用到关于技术的讨论发生在他逝世之后，因此反而愈发增强了其研究的永恒性。值得注意的是，当福柯写出"可见性是一个陷阱"[1]这样的论述时，闭路电视摄像机和因特网还未被发明出来。从这个意义上来说，福柯不可思议地预见了当今世界中关于权力关系的一些重要事实。的确，在过去十年里，围绕数字时代个体隐私而展开的学术及公开辩论，和对新自由主义全球化经济体中权力关系的讨论使得福柯的研究重新获得关注。例如，反资本主义学者迈克尔·哈特*和安东尼奥·内格里*称福柯的作品"为帝国统治的物质功能的研究打开了一扇大门"。[2]此外，左派运动的其他人士将福柯坚持'无绝对的对与错'这一论断视为祸水，称他为"影响其他左派的萎靡之源，是阻碍（行动）的怯懦相对论主义"。[3]

福柯的作品在关于电子监管的讨论中被广泛引用，包括最近大卫·M.贝里的著作《批判理论和数字》（2014），[4]以及辛西娅·韦伯对当代国际关系*理论概要指南的第四版。韦伯简要解释了福柯的观点在数字时代的持久相关性，并且揭示了他的观点对于促使后来爱德华·斯诺登揭发美国政府的监控秘密所起的作用。[5]另外，伊恩·马什和盖纳·梅尔维尔在《犯罪、正义和媒体》（2009）中考察了这些观点的逻辑延伸，讨论了特定信息类型的传播方式（包括对事件的偏见陈述）如何加强和维持社会控制。[6]最后，大卫·莱昂的《监管理论》（2006）一书从福柯的观点出发，将当代社会中的监管角色概念化。该文集中的每位作者都从支持福柯式或反对福柯式的视角审视了监管。[7]

> "可见性是一个陷阱。"
>
> —— 米歇尔·福柯：《规训与惩罚：监狱的诞生》

未来方向

福柯对社会科学的影响在社会学的健康和疾病研究领域尤为显著。特别值得注意的是，健康社会学和疾病社会学在传统意义上一直将身体视为一个"自然的"分析切入点，而福柯将相关的身体和知识视为"构建性的"。实际上，福柯认为从医药角度去理解身体的方式具有历史特殊性。[8] 在这方面运用他的研究就是重新定义该领域的基本研究方法，所以毫不夸张地说，他的研究在这一领域会产生显著的影响。健康社会学领域的泰斗大卫·阿姆斯特朗曾在创作中运用福柯的谱系研究方法，针对医药的主观性、[9] 公共卫生中的身份 [10] 以及医药知识的发展 [11] 这些议题发表了标新立异的看法。

极富影响力的英国社会学家尼古拉斯·罗斯在精神科学方面的创作彰显了他是一个坚定的福柯派学者。[12] 社会学家威廉·雷·阿尼和简·尼尔追溯了对分娩之痛看法的演变，他们称产科医生对于这种疼痛的理解随着"权力—知识"[13] 在疼痛话语中的变化而变化。[14] 堪培拉大学的黛博拉·勒普顿认为那些看起来中性的、不偏不倚的公共卫生措施，实际上充斥着各种意识形态、具有社会主观性并依赖于环境。[15] 这些分析都属于福柯式研究，它们把福柯的谱系学研究方法和他应对权力、监管和主观性的政治—经济法作为出发点。

除社会学外，福柯的思想也影响了城市理论家——他们对市民居住、迁移方式以及监管在这些活动中所起的作用进行研究。福柯也影响了酷儿理论家们，他们研究体制是如何将"传统"观念（如婚姻是异性的结合）根植于人心。福柯认为所有政府都涉及社会建构项目，而强制推行异性恋则是这项目的一部分，以上的学术探究都以此为出发点进行研究。

小结

福柯认为身份不是固定的，权力结构也是依赖情境的，这一历久弥坚的观点对各学科学者们都有裨益。福柯对"规训""权力—知识"[16] 和"监管"等概念的看法也开拓了多情境下理解权力动态学的视角。他的研究有助于更好地理解特定文化议题（如监狱）的含义以及议题的政治意蕴。

福柯对个体和社会整体之间联系的创造性分析，为社会学提供着源源不断的灵感。这一学术分支一直关注认识论意义上关于结构和机构的辩论。虽然福柯的基本理念框架是西式的，他的理论却被运用到了世界各地的研究中，例如，疾病如何与话语体制、而非外部身体（简略来说，就是我们谈论疾病的方式）相联系。[17]

最后，福柯对权力的研究具有永恒性。《规训与惩罚》并非公开批判某一特定团体或组织行使权力。这是一项对某种机制的研究，该机制在个体关系中发挥作用，继而通过这些个体，在社会互动结构中体现。只要人们继续群居生活，这些议题仍将至关重要。

---

1. 米歇尔·福柯：《规训与惩罚：监狱的诞生》，纽约州谢里登：温特吉出版社，1979 年，第 200 页。

2. 迈克尔·哈特和安东尼奥·内格里：《帝国》，马萨诸塞州坎布里奇：哈佛大学出版社，2009 年，第 22 页。

3. 科林·威尔森："米歇尔·福柯：左派的朋友还是敌人？"，《国际社会主义》，2008 年 3 月 31 日。

4. 大卫·M. 贝里：《批判理论和数字》，纽约：布鲁姆斯伯里出版社，2014 年。

5. 辛西娅·韦伯：《国际关系理论：批判性介绍》，第四版，纽约：劳特利奇出版社，2014。参见第 88、140、149、231 页。

6. 伊恩·马什和盖纳·梅尔维尔：《犯罪、正义和媒体》，纽约：劳特利奇出版社，2014 年（2009 年）。

7. 大卫·莱昂:《监管理论》,纽约:劳特利奇出版社,2011 年（2016 年）。

8. 大卫·阿姆斯特朗:"医学中的主体和社会性:解析米歇尔·福柯",《健康和疾病社会学》第 7 卷,1985 年第 1 期,第 111 页。

9. 阿姆斯特朗:"主体和社会性";大卫·阿姆斯特朗:"福柯和健康及疾病社会学",《福柯,健康和医药》,艾伦·彼得森和罗宾·本顿编,伦敦和纽约:劳特利奇出版社,1997 年。

10. 大卫·阿姆斯特朗:"公共卫生空间和身份建构",《社会学》第 27 卷,1993 年第 3 期,第 393—410 页。

11. 大卫·阿姆斯特朗:《政治身体解剖学:20 世纪英国的医药知识》,剑桥:剑桥大学出版社,1983 年。

12. 尼古拉斯·罗斯:《管理灵魂:个体自我的形塑》,肯塔基州佛罗伦萨:泰勒与弗朗西斯出版集团 / 劳特利奇出版社,1990 年。

13. 福柯:《规训与惩罚》,第 27 页。

14. 威廉·雷·阿尼和简·尼尔:"定位分娩中的阵痛:自然分娩和助产术的演变",《健康和疾病社会学》第 4 卷,1982 年第 1 期,第 1—24 页。

15. 黛博拉·勒普顿:《健康的驱动:公共卫生和身体管理》,伦敦;加州千橡市:赛奇出版社,1995 年。

16. 福柯:《规训与惩罚》,第 27 页。

17. 参见斯蒂芬·艾克:"药物公民身份:抗抑郁市场营销和印度的去边缘化前景",《人类学和医药学》第 12 卷,2005 年第 3 期,第 239—254 页。

术语表

1. **管理科学**：治理方式、管理或公共管理的研究，包括对政策、政策如何执行以及管理系统怎样运作的研究。

2. **阿尔及利亚战争**（1954—1962）：法属殖民地阿尔及利亚多个反殖民主义派系与法国之间爆发的战争。反殖民主义者想摆脱法国的统治取得独立。法国和阿尔及利亚两地都燃起了战火，造成了数十万的人员伤亡，其中大多数是阿尔及利亚人。这是两国历史上最惨烈的战争之一，给双方留下了创伤性记忆。

3. **人类学**：研究人类和人类行为及其文化。这一学科吸收了诸如物理、生物、社会科学及人文学科等一系列其他领域的经验知识。

4. **反传统精神病学**：反对传统精神学治疗方法。尽管这一研究方向约有两百年的历史，但是直到 20 世纪 60 年代才得到深入发展，当时政治活动家与学者们开始质疑精神疾病的标准定义并探寻它们发展的过程。

5. **考古学**：通过对史前古器物以及遗迹的分析，来理解过去的人类活动以及昔日社会。在福柯职业生涯的前半段，他在论述自己的历史研究方法时曾提到过该术语：对过去话语及体系所留痕迹的探究，可作为一种途径来理解我们的演变过程。

6. **布雷顿森林体系**：一种货币管理制度，在 20 世纪中期起到了管理主要工业经济体间商业和金融关系的作用。

7. **监狱类**：与拘留所、监狱以及其他类似机构有关的。

8. **监狱连续体**：这一术语被福柯用来定义现代社会对规训和惩罚措施的依赖。不仅是监狱和少管所，学校、工厂、办公室以及医院都使用监狱式措施来巩固他们的制度。"连续体"这一术语指的是这些不同机构对惩罚对象所施加的措施尽管等级不同，但都体现了在催生服从性方面的统一。连续体最大的成果在于使惩罚的权力合法化：我们认为老师、医生以及雇主对我们进行评判是理所当然的。

9. **闭路电视（CCTV）**：这一术语指的是通过电视摄像机来对公共或私人场所进行监控。被广泛应用于银行、商店以及机场等场所，机构或政府比较关注在这类场所中人们的行为表现。

10. **胁迫**：违背某人意愿，操控其做事的行为。

11. **殖民主义**：外国主宰势力在某领土上对殖民地的创建和管理。在欧洲殖民时期，从 16 世纪一直延续到 20 世纪，欧洲势力在亚洲、非洲及美洲建立了广阔的殖民地，产生了深远的影响。

12. **交际理性**：有影响力的社会学家尤尔根·哈贝马斯发明的术语。哈贝马斯借鉴的理论是：理性是个体间成功沟通的产物。

13. **偶然性**：哲学术语，被用来表示某具体提议不具普适性，或并不总是正确的，它的真实性实际上依赖其他因素。例如，当福柯称某事物具有历史偶然性时，指的是它的发生源于某个特定历史情境，它发生的情况可能完全不同，或根本不会发生。

14. **犯罪学**：在个体及社会层面上，对犯罪及越轨行为的起因、本质、定义和预防的研究。

15. **文化研究**：这一学科领域研究文化现象，诸如阶级结构、意识形态、国家形成、性以及种族感知，所运用到的一系列不同理论方法涵盖了人类学、政治科学和社会学。这一研究是建立在认为文化非固定的设想之上，而把文化发展看作一个不断演变的过程，易受更广泛的社会经济、政治及历史性变化的影响，同时文化也反映了这些变化。

16. **网络监控**：以硬件或软件为工具对某个体或团体的计算机或网络活动的监控，可能开展这一活动的机构范围广泛，包括雇主、企业以及政府。

17. **非人化**：通过使某个人或某几个人看起来不人道，使其不值得拥有人道待遇从而妖魔化他们的系统过程。非人化是诸如战争之类事件的中心情境，因为它为杀戮开脱；又比如殖民主义，因为它为剥夺人权及靠暴力剥夺权利的行为提供了辩护。

18. **数字文化 / 数字文化研究**：当代文化中的新媒体和新兴媒体设备以及对它们的研究。

19. **规训**：正如《规训与惩罚》中所示，一种施加权力的机制。它不是权力本身，而是指鼓励个体进行自我管理的多种途径，诸如使用时间表、空间组织及演练等来鼓励特定形式的身体行为。

20. **话语 / 话语实践 / 话语机制**：福柯将其看作话语的一种方式，视其为历史与权力的产物。话语实践是通过一系列规则告知在特定的时间和地点的个体所能采取的话语方式。"话语机制"这一术语指的是话语方式中交叠的权力，其中有些话语可以说，也有些话语不能说。

21. **计量经济**：与把数据理论或方法运用到经济数据上有关或以此为特征。

22. **经济学**：社会科学的一个学术领域，探究经济系统、结构、政策、趋势以及它们对商品和服务的生产、分配和消费的影响。

23. **解放**：先前被剥夺权利的团体获得了社会、经济以及 / 或者政治权利。

24. **启蒙时代**：也被称为理性时代，大约从 1650 年延续到 1780 年，期间西欧文化和思想逐渐从宗教信仰转而重视个人主义、理性和分析。这一时期鲜明的观点是理性思想可以战胜任何歧义，而逻辑可以解决世界上的谜团。

25. **认识论**：这一哲学的分支是关于知识的本质，致力于理解我们如何"知道"我们知道什么。

26. **存在主义**：这一哲学的分支认为个体（与社会、国家和宗教对立）是意义、秩序以及道德的基础。

27. **女权主义**：与妇女们平等的社会、政治、文化和经济权利相关的一系列思想观念运动，包括在家庭、工作场所、教育方面以及政府中的平等权利。

28. **谱系学**：从字面上说，指关于家族世系及历史的研究。不过，福柯在提及《规训与惩罚》中的历史研究法时使用了这一术语并延续至今。他将其与自己先前的考古学研究法区分开，称虽然两种方法都探究知识体系与话语的历史，谱系学追溯了权力在这些体系中所扮演的角色，并判定某事物为"真"、其他为"假"。

29. **全球化**：不同国家间政府、人种及公司的融合与互动的过程。这一过程由国际贸易和投资所带动，受信息技术的推动。

30. **治理术**：这一术语在福柯的《规训与惩罚》以及他的最后一本著作《性史》中被用来定义两种事物：现代欧洲中紧随国家诞生而出现的一种特定人口管理形式，以及之后用来治理人口和个体的所有系统与机制，包括自我管理形式。

31. **历史**：这一学术领域致力于研究与解释历史事件和它们的意义，包括研究不同文化与不同年代人对同一事件的理解差异。

32. **人道主义**：这一哲学的分支倾向于强调普遍人性和人类天性的重要性，将其视为意义与道德的来源，而非社会或宗教。

33. **人力资源管理**：某一公司的分支或部门，负责监管员工纪律与商业运作（因他们对公司产能的贡献被视为人力资源）。这一部门把控从业人员的技能和资格，管理薪资、福利以及休假。

34. **国际关系**：研究国际治理体系。该领域的学者可能会探究诸如国家、国际组织、非政府组织以及跨国企业等作用物间的关系。

35. **伊朗伊斯兰革命**（1979）：也被称为1979年革命或伊斯兰革命，当时一系列旨在推翻国家压迫式君主制度的起义达到了高潮，很多人认为君主是西方的傀儡，并被西方价值观过度影响。事件开始于1978年，受伊朗左派的煽动及数次学生运动的影响，最终导致了伊斯兰共和国的建立。该共和国将自身与西方的资本主义价值观以及苏联的共产主义价值观脱离开。福柯是这场革命的坚定支持者。

36. **文学研究／文学批评**：对文学的评价、研究和解释。

37. **马克思主义**：以19世纪政治经济学家卡尔·马克思的著作为基石，是一场关于文化、哲学、社会经济、政治和美学的运动。马克思主义理论家和作家们关注资本主义下滋生的社会不公以及它对文化和社会的影响。

38. **唯物主义**：这一学术流派认为物质是塑造社会及历史趋势的关键因素。例如，卡尔·马克思称社会变化的关键催化剂是人们满足自身物质需求方式的变化。

39. **媒体研究**：这一学术领域探究新媒体的内容、文化效应及历史，特别是大众传媒，比如电视、广播和电影。该领域将文艺评论和艺术史（体现在对特定形式的媒体和它们的内容的分析上）与社会学、政治科学以及历史相结合（体现在探究催生了特定媒体形式的社会文化情境，以及这些形式对内容的影响）。

40. **现代性**：人文学科和社会科学中使用的术语，一般指 16 世纪到 20 世纪早期这段时期，以反对传统观念著称。

41. **新自由主义**：一系列鼓励经济自由化、自由贸易、开放市场、私有化、放宽管制以及强化私营部门角色的经济政策。

42. **常态化**：在社会学领域，该术语指的是关于行为模式的特定观念成为惯例的过程。不过，福柯将这一术语和机构性权力对生成从众性所产生的影响联系在了一起：也就是说，惩戒性的政权如何在公民中催生从众性来去除反常或越轨行为。现代惩戒性权力的力量来源于其进行有效社会控制的能力（使用最少的资源），使人们保持一致并遵守规则。

43. **国家安全局（NSA）**：美国政府机构，负责监管可能波及美国国家安全利益的信息与个人。2013 年，美国"吹哨人"爱德华·斯诺登极具争议性地公布了国家安全局秘密监听项目的细节。

44. **组织社会学**：社会学的这一分支探究了现代组织的内部功能以及它们更加广泛的社会角色。这可能包括机构如何进行劳动分工、分配资源或应对变化。

45. **全景敞视主义**：关于监狱模式的理论，运用全景式监狱的叙述视角及它促使个体进行自我管理的能力，成为社会中所有权力关系的典范。

46. **全景式监狱**：英国社会改革家杰里米·边沁提出的关于监狱的一个概念。设计这一结构是为使单个狱警能够对大批囚犯进行无形监视。认为他们正在被监视的想法会使囚犯们管制自身行为，并有效进行自我管理，从而使得现场狱警的存在变得不必要。

47. **五月风暴（1968 年巴黎起义）**：一场社会动乱，由工人罢工、示威以及学生占领大学教学楼等学潮所主导。

48. **刑罚学**：犯罪学的这一分支研究惩罚和刑罚制度的理论、措施和有效性。

49. **现象学**：一种哲学研究方法，考察形塑个体经验和个体知觉的结构。在心理学领域，这一路径被用来研究主体经验。

50. **哲学**：人文学科的这一领域研究的是与现实、知识、存在、理性、语言以及价值观念相关的基本人类问题。

51. **政治科学**：社会科学的这一领域研究政府政策和政治活动，以及国家、政府和政权的动态。

52. **后结构主义**：哲学的这一领域兴起于 20 世纪 70 年代，作为对结构主义的刻板印象与历史相对主论的回击。后结构主义学者们认为结构主义不能解释知识自身的不稳定性：知识的结构是社会性的构造，这就意味着我们永远无法摆脱尝试理解的机制的自身束缚。后结构主义者们称所有形式的知识在关于真理的构成的特定设想上是依情况而定的。依次类推，对于文本、历史事件或想法的任何解释，只要其作为前提的信条被质疑，那么这些解释就会顷刻间被否定。尽管福柯拒绝被定义为后结构主义者，但是他的很多观点都属于这一范畴。

53. **权力—知识**：这一术语由福柯提出，用来表示知识永远由权力构成而反之亦然；换句话说，去"认识"某人，将他们归类，就是对他们施展权力。

54. **精神病学**：医学的这一分支专攻对精神、情感以及行为失常的研究、治疗和预防。

55. **心理学**：学术及应用学科，关于心理行为和心理机能的研究和治疗。

56. **酷儿理论**：后结构主义理论的一个广阔领域，与性少数群体（女同性恋、男同性恋、双性恋及跨性别者）和女性研究相联系，并深入其中探究：什么才是"正常"的，什么又是离经叛道。

57. **理性**：保持理智的状态，即依循个人的理性信念去认知和行动。理性思想基于理性和逻辑，自启蒙运动后成为社会学家和哲学家们探索的主体。

58. **凝视（Le regard）**：这一术语被福柯用来描述可见性在现代权力与知识

体系中的角色。无论是国家、学校行政、医院职工、狱警还是公司领导所实施的机构监督，都使机制中的主体得以正常化，也就是说，它驱使机制内的人们遵从标准，这不仅体现在遵守法律上，也体现在按照机制的意愿来行事和思考。福柯称凝视使个体进行自我修正：在机构监督之下，我们成了因为害怕被发现、评判或惩罚而避免做某事的总和。

59. **社会学**：关于社会行为的学术研究。这一学科探究社会关系的起源和发展、它们不同的组织形式以及不同的社会机构。

60. **法律社会学**：社会学的这一分支从理论和实证的角度来探究法律的产生和实施，以及在协调社会关系方面法律机构所起的作用。一些学者将之视为法律研究的分支，又或者将它看作结合了社会学及法律因素的一个领域。

61. **刑罚社会学**：社会学的这一分支，专攻我们进行惩罚的原因及方式，包括惩罚的深层原因、特定惩罚形式的实施及随之产生的效果。

62. **结构主义**：一门哲学及社会学思想学派，在 20 世纪五六十年代盛行，也被看作是对存在主义人文主义的反驳。人类学家克洛德·列维－斯特劳斯和精神分析学家雅克·拉康是结构主义的主要支持者。这些学者们强调人类经验、文化和知识是更为宽泛的、潜在的意识形态、社会文化和经济结构作用下的产物；我们的自我认知以及我们对世界的理解是特定社会建构的产物。当这一学派诞生时，它常被视为马克思主义的直接反对者。结构主义常和福柯联系起来，但是他本人拒绝被划入这一分类。

63. **压迫**：征服并控制某人或某物，并且使其服从。

64. **监视**：对行为进行监视，通常是为了控制、改变或是进行操纵。

65. **极权主义**：政府的一种制度，国家对社会的方方面面有着绝对控制。纳粹德国是极权国家的代表。

66. **越南战争**（1955—1975）：也被称为第二次印度支那战争，冲突爆发于北越和南越之间，战场波及老挝、柬埔寨和越南。因互相竞争的全球大国在其中扮演的角色，这场战争也被归为冷战时期的冲突。

67. **福利国家**：社会或政府组织的一种制度，包含了为公民提供保障以及倡导福利。公共教育以及全民医疗保险都是社会福利的范例。

人名表

1. C. 弗雷德·阿尔福德（1947年生），政治心理学家，曾开创性地在文章中批判福柯对监狱生活的论述。

2. 路易·阿尔都塞（1918—1990），法国马克思主义哲学家，与当今的结构主义学派有着密切的联系。然而，阿尔都塞对部分结构主义者的思想体系存批判态度，他穷尽一生致力于支持马克思主义核心信条。

3. 齐格蒙特·鲍曼（1925—2017），波兰社会主义学家，世界上最重要的社会思想家之一。他的作品涉及题材广泛，从大屠杀、理性、现代性到消费主义。他是利兹大学的社会学名誉教授。

4. 西蒙娜·德·波伏娃（1908—1986），可能是20世纪最著名、最具影响力的女性哲学家和作家。她以存在主义女性主义和女权主义思想方面的著作而闻名。

5. 杰里米·边沁（1748—1832），英国社会改革家，以其对法律哲学的贡献、对废奴及废除死刑的倡导以及对政教分离的激烈观点而闻名。他对全景监狱的构想虽然从未真正实现，但是对后世的思想家产生了巨大影响，其中就包括福柯。

6. 埃米尔·杜尔凯姆（1858—1917），法国社会学家、哲学家。他一般被认为是社会学的奠基人。杜尔凯姆的作品大多关系社会向"现代性"的过渡——这一时期的特点是教会的力量开始衰落，技术获得新发展，城市不断壮大。他以《社会分工论》（1893）一书中对社会组织的研究以及对犯罪的研究著作而闻名。

7. 南希·弗雷泽（1947年生），政治哲学家，以对"正义"这一概念的大量写作而著称。她是最早对福柯思想进行广泛研究的英语学者之一。

8. 尤尔根·哈贝马斯（1929年生），备受尊敬的社会科学家和哲学家。他和福柯就理性的质量和解放的潜力产生了意见冲突。他是当代作者中对启蒙运动推崇的理性主义最强有力的捍卫者，与福柯对理性的批判，认为其是文化和偶然的产物这一观点形成了鲜明对比。

9. **迈克尔·哈特**（1960年生），美国政治哲学家以及文学理论家，以其和安东尼奥·内格里的合著《帝国》（2000）以及《群众》（2004）而著称。

10. **格奥尔格·威廉·弗里德里希·黑格尔**（1770—1831），德国哲学家以及理想主义运动中的重要人物。他以对现实的历史主义者及现实主义者视角论述而著名。他的"系统"概念，即心智与自然、主体与客体等之间的集成，是首个承认这一系统间存在矛盾与对立的创举之一。

11. **让·伊波利特**（1907—1968），法国哲学家、格奥尔格·黑格尔和德国哲学运动的追随者、20世纪中叶法国思想界的著名人物。福柯师从于他，并深受其对于历史与哲学间关系看法的影响。

12. **卡尔·马克思**（1818—1983），德国政治学家和经济学家，他对资本主义之下的阶级关系进行了分析并呼吁建立为共产主义提供基石的平均主义体制。马克思与弗里德里希·恩格斯一起合著了《共产党宣言》（1848）。他在《资本论》（1867—1894）一书中阐述了生产和阶级关系的全部理论。

13. **莫里斯·梅洛-庞蒂**（1908—1961），法国现象学哲学家、作家。庞蒂是他的时代里唯一将描述心理学融入作品中的重要哲学家。这也影响了后世的现象学家们，他们继续在研究中运用了认知科学和心理学。

14. **安东尼奥·内格里**（1933年生），杰出的意大利马克思主义政治哲学家和活动家。以其和迈克尔·哈特的合著《帝国》（2000）以及《群众》（2004）而著称。

15. **弗里德里希·尼采**（1844—1900），激进的德国哲学家、文字学家、诗人以及文化评论家。他的作品对西方哲学有重要影响。他以对"上帝已死"的观点、对道德的论述以及对真理的客观性探寻而著称。

16. **尼古拉斯·罗斯**（1947 年生），具影响力的英国社会理论家和社会学家。他对心理健康政策与风险、精神病学中的社会学与历史、心理健康领域精神药理学新发展的社会影响等方面都有著述。他以对福柯的论述以及在英语世界重燃对福柯关于治理性概念的兴趣而闻名。

17. **让-保罗·萨特**（1905—1980），法国存在主义哲学家、20 世纪法国哲学和马克思主义学派重要思想家。他的作品，包括小说和戏剧在内都以个体是"注定要受自由之苦"，不存在创造者的这些观点为内核。

18. **爱德华·斯诺登**（1983 年生），美国电脑专家，他因 2013 年 6 月泄露美国国家安全局的机密信息而广为人知。他的泄密揭露了美国等国家与一些全球电信公司合作的全球监管机制运作，引发了关于国家安全和个人隐私的讨论。

19. **芭芭拉·汤利**（1954 年生），社会学家、社会理论家，以其关于福柯的著作和管理学研究而闻名，其管理研究包括了对高等教育、政府和文化产业中业绩评估的运用。

WAYS IN TO THE TEXT

KEY POINTS

- Michel Foucault (1926–84) was a French social philosopher and historian.

- *Discipline and Punish* proposes a theory of modern power relations — the power held by different sections of society — by tracing a history of the modern prison and its impact on other social institutions such as hospitals, factories, schools, and workplaces.

- *Discipline and Punish* has had an impact on the approach taken by scholars in the humanities and social sciences in understanding power, through its investigation of the roles of surveillance* — systematic monitoring — and knowledge-creation in constructing both individuals and relationships.

Who Was Michel Foucault?

Michel Foucault, the author of *Discipline and Punish: The Birth of the Prison* (1975), was a radical French social philosopher, historian, and literary critic. Today, he is widely recognized as being one of the most influential contemporary thinkers in both the social sciences and the humanities.

The son of a surgeon, Foucault grew up in a wealthy and socially conservative home in western France, and enjoyed a privileged education. Against his father's wishes, he studied philosophy* and the history of science at university, and wrote his PhD thesis on the history of madness. In it, he drew a distinction between mental illness and madness; the latter, he argued, is a social construct based on subjective assumptions.

The thesis was published in English as *Madness and Civilization* and later as *History of Madness*. It was extremely well received, winning the prestigious Medal of the Centre national de la recherche scientifique (the French National Center for Scientific Research), the main governmental research organization in France. Foucault's next books were *The Birth of the Clinic* (1963), *The Order of Things* (1966), and *The Archaeology of Knowledge* (1969).

Throughout his life, Foucault remained committed to left-wing politics: he was, for example, a leading anti-prison activist. Much French left-wing activism in the 1960s and 1970s was dominated by certain Marxist* ideas — that is, beliefs derived from the work of the German political theorist Karl Marx* — about the need to end structures of power that exploited wage earners and others. Foucault's intellectual contributions, however, were based on his claim that no one person or group alone possesses power: as the individual is constructed from the power relations in which he or she lives, escape from those power relations is impossible.

What Does *Discipline and Punish* Say?

In *Discipline and Punish*, Foucault departs from the idea of power as something exerted by the government, by a king, or by those with material wealth. Power, he says, is "discipline."* It is important to note the particular way in which Foucault uses the word, however; for him, discipline is not the top-down application of direct coercion* but power used in a way that makes the individual self-regulate.

Taking the penal system as an example, he demonstrates how the discipline of the prison is a specific form of power that has become embedded in society since its emergence in the seventeenth century. It is, in other words, "historically contingent,"* meaning it grew out of a particular historical context.

Beyond the history of such disciplinary procedures, Foucault is concerned with the techniques and mechanisms of power that use these approaches. In this work, Foucault begins a deep examination of the relationship between the physical body, the individual, and what he calls "power-knowledge"*[1] — the marriage of power and knowledge that allows the powerful to classify and control people and things. These are all themes that appear throughout his writings.

Discipline and Punish argues that social institutions exercise power and discipline on the bodies and souls of their subjects through *le regard** — the "gaze."[2] Forming this argument, he turns to a discussion of the Panopticon,* a model for a prison invented by the British social reformer Jeremy Bentham* in the late eighteenth century. The Panopticon was designed so that the inmates cannot see their guards and, therefore, never know if they are being watched or not; it is the perpetual possibility of observation that encourages them to behave. Foucault suggests that the Panopticon and the mechanisms of power it contains extend beyond the prison and into other institutions of society (a driver who cannot be certain that she or he is not being tracked by a speed camera, for example, may choose not to speed "just in case"). According to this view, behavior is conditioned by the awareness of the possibility of control.

For Foucault, the individual is essentially a product of this monitoring and control. Surveillance — systematic monitoring — by government institutions produces "docile bodies,"[3] which

Foucault defines as bodies that can be monitored and psychologically controlled, and which are then trained to self-govern. Put simply, we are the sum of what we abstain from doing for fear of being seen, judged, or punished.

Why Does *Discipline and Punish* Matter?

Discipline and Punish is considered one of the modern classics of sociological, historical, and philosophical thought. The groundbreaking analysis of power that Foucault presents in his study of social institutions has produced important insights into how individuals and masses are governed. It traces the evolution of modern power structures — such as current prison systems — and considers their effects on human freedom and identity. *Discipline and Punish* is also unique in its approach to its argument: it is not so much a theory of power as a history of its transformation. Foucault's historical approach was designed to allow for the study of different institutions and power structures; the work itself was not intended as a critique of any one specific system, but was, rather, a way to understand how power itself works.

Foucault's analyses encouraged scholars to dramatically re-evaluate how they view the operation of power, knowledge, and what constitutes the individual. Even though some sociologists may not agree with Foucault's understanding of power, there are few trained sociologists who are unfamiliar with it.

Discipline and Punish has had an impact on other disciplines as well. Foucault's recognition that individuals are shaped by the systems of power and knowledge they inhabit has been widely applied in academic debates about human agency and choice and in discussions about identity. The Foucauldian understanding of power and concepts such as discourse* (for Foucault, a way of speaking arising from the influence of history and power — but a term often used for the exchange of ideas, and the way that this exchange defines how something is understood), "power-knowledge,"4 and panopticism* (the theory that the Panopticon prison is a model for all power relations in society), for example, have not only become part of the vocabulary of sociology,* but appear in disciplines as diverse as history,* economics,* anthropology,* and political science.*

Scholars in fields as varied as cultural studies*, media studies,* and literary studies* have applied Foucault's ideas to the analysis of power relations in literature, music, film, and television. The theory advanced in *Discipline and Punish* is often used to understand how individuals internalize power, and the effect this has on both social relations and the possibility of resistance.

Foucault's ideas have gained new relevance in current debates on individual privacy in the digital age. His identification of the practical benefits of surveillance for social institutions, as well as its human toll, anticipated many of the discussions we have today about the effects of living under the gaze of closed circuit TV (CCTV)* cameras. Similarly, the disclosures made in 2013 by the whistle-blower Edward Snowden,* revealing the extent of the surveillance of US citizens conducted by the state agency known as the National Security Agency (NSA),* in many ways confirm aspects of Foucault's thesis.

1. Michel Foucault, *Discipline and Punish*: *The Birth of the Prison* (Sheridan, NY: Vintage Books, 1979), 27.
2. Foucault, *Discipline and Punish*, 96.
3. Foucault, *Discipline and Punish*, 135.
4. Foucault, *Discipline and Punish*, 27.

SECTION 1
INFLUENCES

THE AUTHOR AND THE HISTORICAL CONTEXT

KEY POINTS

* Michel Foucault's text, with its novel ideas about power, has been a key work for a range of academic disciplines. It continues to be relevant, as new concerns arise about such issues as state surveillance* of public areas and the Internet.

* Foucault's ideas were shaped by his early experiences, especially his repressive upbringing (being gay), his personal experiences of the French psychiatric system, and his involvement with prison reform groups.

* Foucault's beliefs were also formed by his involvement in radical left-wing French politics and the students' riots of 1968, which had a deep effect on French thought and society.

Why Read This Text?

Michel Foucault's *Discipline and Punish: The Birth of the Prison* (1975) is a key text for a number of different disciplines, including sociology* (the study of the history and structure of societies), philosophy* (the study of fundamental human problems related to reality, knowledge and existence), and history.* It offers a unique analysis of the evolution of power and modern power structures. In doing so, it asks its readers to rethink taken-for-granted ideas about the nature of power, reason, and the formation of the individual.

Historians are still reading *Discipline and Punish* because of Foucault's claims about history. Criminologists (scholars of matters relating to crime and criminal behavior) are still reading the text because of Foucault's theories about the development and workings of modern prisons. Philosophers are still reading the text because of what it says about the nature of reason and rationality.* And scholars interested in power, from various fields and disciplines, are still reading the text because of the radically new way it looked at the nature of modern power. Given the long-lasting questions about power, the nature of reason, the role of punishment in society, and the forms in which punishment takes, it is unlikely that *Discipline and Punish* will lose its relevancy in the near future. Concerns about the use and abuse of surveillance techniques, such as the explosion of video cameras monitoring public places and cyberveillance* (monitoring of Internet use), has given the text new relevance.

> *"I'm not making a problem out of a personal question; I make of a personal question an absence of a problem."*
> —— Michel Foucault, *The Chomsky-Foucault Debate*

Author's Life

Michel Foucault (1926–84) grew up in a wealthy, socially conservative family in France. Foucault's father was a surgeon, and pushed his son to follow in his footsteps. Foucault resisted, and instead went to the Lycée Henri-IV, an elite public high school in Paris, where he studied philosophy under Jean Hyppolite* — an expert on the nineteenth-century philosopher Hegel.* In 1946, Foucault entered the École normale supérieure (ENS) in Paris, the most prestigious humanities university in France, where he studied under the influential Marxist* philosopher Louis Althusser.* He received a degree in psychology in 1948 and a second degree in philosophy in 1951, working with the equally influential philosopher Maurice Merleau-Ponty,* noted for his work in the field of phenomenology* — roughly, a philosophical approach that emphasizes the nature and role of perception in the formation of consciousness.

Foucault admitted throughout his career that his life story had a strong influence on the books he wrote: notably his sexuality and his personal experiences with madness and prison systems. Foucault was gay and his early career was framed by the repression of his sexual identity. In 1948, he attempted suicide and received psychiatric treatment in Paris. Doctors diagnosed later suicide attempts as his reaction to the social shame attached to being openly gay in a society that saw homosexuality as a curse.

Foucault's concern with power, madness, and sexuality turns up again and again in his writings. His first book, *Madness and Civilization* (1961), dealt with psychiatry,* a practice with which he had been closely involved both as a patient and later, in the 1950s, as a researcher in a psychiatric hospital. Both psychology* and phenomenology, the subjects of his first two university degrees, are ever-present in the theory and approach of his books. Moreover, his social identity and concern about oppression can be seen throughout his work.

Foucault's political involvement increased in the early 1970s, when he helped found the Prison Information Group, which attempted to focus the attention of the press and the public on prison conditions. We must thank this period of political activism and Foucault's writing on disciplinary institutions for the eventual production of *Discipline and Punish*.

Author's Background

Foucault wrote *Discipline and Punish* at a time of intense sociocultural and political upheaval. France in the 1960s saw a number of conflicts. These included opposition to the country's role in the Vietnam War* (a war fought in Laos, Cambodia, and Vietnam between 1955 and 1975), its treatment of its colonies (and the colonial* system itself), and the structure of its education system. Critics attacked the latter for placing the children of the rich in schools that prepared them for the best jobs. There were also deep anti-capitalist feelings, which gave rise to strikes and occupations of university buildings and factories across the country.

This unrest peaked with the Paris Riots of 1968,* which saw university students occupy the Sorbonne, one of Europe's most distinguished universities, to protest against the capitalist system and "traditional" values, and a two-week general strike involving 11 million workers during which the French economy basically ground to a halt. The government itself stopped functioning when the country's president secretly fled for a few hours. This period had a deep impact on French society, and was viewed as a watershed moment.

This context provides an important key to understanding the origins of Foucault's work: as well as being a scholar, Foucault

89

was active in various left-wing movements. He was involved in anti-colonialist efforts, including supporting the Algerian war* for independence from French rule (1954–62), and in the anti-psychiatry movement* of the 1960s, which opposed practices such as electroshock treatment and lobotomy (a now discredited treatment for mental illness that involved partly destroying the frontal lobes of the brain). He also supported the Iranian Revolution* of 1978, writing articles for the Italian newspaper *Corriere della Sera* and for the French news magazine *Le Nouvel Observateur*. His interest, however, was in the power dynamics playing out rather than in the political interests of any one party. Foucault's concern with the revolution was with its capacity to undermine and then remove the previous Iranian government and power, rather than with the system that would replace the country's monarchy.

Foucault's critiques of colonial oppression, totalitarianism* (a system of government in which the citizen is fully subject to the power of the state), and psychiatry go hand in hand with his views on sexual repression and the "power-knowledge"* complex — the way those in power control information or knowledge. If, on the surface, *Discipline and Punish* is a history of the modern prison and modern methods of punishment, it is also a critique of modern society's ability to encourage or force individuals into self-regulation and conformity.

MODULE 2
ACADEMIC CONTEXT

KEY POINTS

* Foucault came of age at a time when left-wing thought was dominated by the philosophical approaches known as existentialism* and phenomenology,* and the economic and social analytical methods of Marxism.* Challenging those ideas, he moved close to "poststructuralist"* thought with his arguments that human identity is socially and historically constructed.

* Foucault attacked the leading French philosopher Jean-Paul Sartre,* criticizing him for focusing too much on the individual, and not enough on the wider system that molds the individual.

* Influenced by the German philosopher Friedrich Nietzsche,* Foucault believed that rationality,* punishment, and power are not fixed ideas, but rather, they develop out of the history of any particular society.

The Work in Its Context

Michel Foucault described his book *Discipline and Punish* as a "history of the modern soul."[1] The work marked a sharp departure from both the Marxism that dominated left-wing political thought at the time and structuralism* (the position that the analysis of human experience and culture requires the identification of ideological, sociocultural, and economic structures underlying them). The key philosophical movements during Foucault's youth were existentialism (a philosophical approach that emphasizes the experience and nature of the human individual), phenomenology (a study that focuses on the nature and role of perception in the formation of consciousness), and Marxism (an understanding of social and political processes founded, very roughly, on a critical analysis of capitalism). These three movements were united by their "humanist"* core, especially the belief that action is determined by human nature, and class or social inequality, rather than by God.

In the 1950s and 1960s, these approaches were challenged by structuralism, a theory that says human activity and thought are socially constructed through language. Structuralists believe that the meaning we give to particular events, moments, people, and activities is entirely based on our belief system, historical context, cultural background, and language. Foucault built on this idea, but took it further. He associated himself with poststructuralism* by claiming that individual identity and meaning are not fixed, but are subject to interpretation depending on one's circumstance and perspective (the position from which you are viewing things).

Poststructuralists would argue that texts can be understood in the same way. Their meaning is contingent* on — that is, it depends on — circumstance, perspective, and time. A book, a political speech, or another text might be interpreted in many different ways, and these interpretations are entirely contingent upon the reader. In this approach, Foucault would argue that knowledge and identity are socially constructed: they are not natural, being the product of social norms, belief, or customs. This understanding can then be extended to the prison system, which, similarly, is not a basic, fixed part of society, but a practice that is changeable.

> "The 'Enlightenment', which discovered the liberties, also invented the disciplines."
>
> —— Michel Foucault, *Discipline and Punish: The Birth of the Prison*

Overview of the Field

The philosophers who contributed the most to the schools of thought identified above were the philosophers Maurice Merleau-Ponty* and Jean-Paul Sartre. These thinkers did not so much influence Foucault directly as shape the fields in which he worked, and create ideas that Foucault ended up rejecting. Along with the phenomenologist Merleau-Ponty, Foucault was concerned with individual, subjective, and bodily experience, and emphasized the importance of this type of experience in understanding the political and social world. Merleau-Ponty's philosophy approached the universal human condition through the body and the way the body sees and feels the world, and the order and meaning it gives to what it perceives. Foucault, however, rejected the idea of a universal human experience of the world.

Sartre's work provides an important context to Foucault's intellectual growth and philosophical approach. Both Sartre and Foucault sympathized with marginalized groups, such as ethnic minorities, homosexuals, and prisoners. These feelings inspired them to political activism. Foucault distanced himself, however, from Sartre's philosophical work, and often argued against Sartre's views. Although they shared some ideas, it is useful to see their projects as separate, even in opposition. Foucault criticized Sartre's emphasis of the individual experience, terming it "transcendental narcissism." By this, Foucault meant that Sartre placed too much importance on the individual subject and too little importance on the system(s) in which individuals find themselves. The "transcendental narcissism" insult was an attack on the way Sartre put the individual at the center of the system, as opposed to accepting that the individual is constructed by the system.

By rejecting the idea of a universal human nature, Foucault was seen as close to structuralism and poststructuralism. Structuralism shares similar concerns to Foucault's — namely, how individuals develop their identities through language. And poststructuralism's idea that entities such as a text or an action can have a variety of interpretations is close to Foucault's understanding of the way knowledge and knowledge systems can be shaped and pushed in different directions.

Academic Influences

Although Foucault's academic influences were many and varied, it can certainly be said that structuralism, poststructuralism, and the work of the nineteenth-century German philosopher Friedrich Nietzsche had a big impact on him.

Foucault's analysis of the development of the prison as a product of wider structural and historical forces suggests the influence of structuralist thinking. The structuralist approach sees individual people as molded by their institutions (school, for example, or the legal system). Foucault did not take the institution of the prison or the individual as a given but, rather, focused on how they were created. The influence of poststructuralism can also be seen in Foucault's claim, throughout *Discipline and Punish*, that the penal system has multiple meanings: it can be both a good and a repressive force.

Foucault, however, rejected his placement within these schools of thought. He insisted that the text's use of a method he called "genealogy"* was its main contribution. It is here that Nietzsche's influence is clear, particularly his studies of morality. Foucault's project on the "genealogy of knowledge"[2] is a direct reference to Nietzsche's concept of a "genealogy of morals."[3] Nietzsche did not take morality as a given, but tried, rather, to account for the ways in which the historical context shapes the values and morals that we have.

This approach influenced the claim Foucault makes in *Discipline and Punish* that our ideas about rationality, punishment, and power inherited from the Enlightenment* (the period of European intellectual history, roughly 1650 to 1780, in which rational thought and behavior were emphasized over religion and superstition) are similarly historically contingent and that one can trace their evolution.

Genealogy can be understood as a style of inquiry that attempts to explain the present by looking to the past; it attempts to trace how we got from "there" to "here." For Foucault, it was genealogy that produced his insights about the nature of discipline* and power, and how they served to construct the self.

1. Michel Foucault, *Discipline and Punish: The Birth of the Prison* (Sheridan, NY: Vintage Books, 1979), 23.

2. Foucault, *Discipline and Punish*, 27.

3. Friedrich Wilhelm Nietzsche, *The Genealogy of Morals* (London and New York: Macmillan, 1897).

MODULE 3
THE PROBLEM

KEY POINTS

* Foucault's work explores how the norms of proper behavior, rationality, and the exercise of power are based on the historical context, and change over time.

* His approach angered many other philosophers, who felt that the aim of their discipline was to search for universal truths.

* Foucault tries to show that power in society has evolved to control and punish "bad" behavior in more subtle and widespread ways than in the past. However, he rejects the common idea that we have been steadily marching toward a more rational system.

Core Question

In *Discipline and Punish*, Michel Foucault sought to understand how the modern individual came to be and how modern forms of power differed from older forms. His project was not merely a description of a certain modern type of power but was, rather, an explanation of how that form of power came to be.

Foucault did this by focusing on the changing relationship between the human body and power; this changing relationship, he argued, effected the operations of power in general. Whereas the body used to be something to be punished corporally, by means of public torture or even death, now the body is something acted upon by way of norms, corrections, and regulations. Foucault was concerned with the ways in which the individual became the target and the product of power. This occurs through the communication of norms for behavior, which the individual is supposed to accept.

Through this, Foucault wanted to show that there is a relationship between power and knowledge. Institutional power — the power of the schools and the justice system, for example — and the construction of knowledge are deeply connected, and, according to Foucault, together they shape individuals' desires and the way they understand their place in the world. Every social norm, every impulse that society takes for granted, Foucault sought to show, is historically produced and contingent upon the systems of knowledge that created it. Power rests in the production of what is "normal." Individuals want to be "normal," and so they act in accordance with these norms.

> *"There is no power relation without the correlative constitution of a field of knowledge, nor any knowledge that does not presuppose and constitute at the same time power relations."*
> —— Michel Foucault, *Discipline and Punish: The Birth of the Prison*

The Participants

While other scholars studied institutions or social structures, Foucault termed himself a historian of systems of thought. He took as his unit of analysis the language that shapes social reality — in essence, he attempts to understand the language and thinking that create different systems of thought. This was a novel approach to understanding history, leading him into largely uncharted territory.

Foucault angered many philosophers with this approach, since the main concern of philosophy is generally considered to be with universal truths — that is, with the study of knowledge that is valid in all times and places. In this sense, philosophy* is understood to be independent of history and culture. Foucault argued against this by placing language and thought in particular social, cultural, and historical contexts, and his strongest critics were those who objected to these premises.

Among his best-known critics was the German sociologist Jürgen Habermas.* Foucault also faced intense objections from Marxist* philosophers who approached power from a materialist* point of view — that is, they saw power as the result of social inequality and the uneven distribution of wealth. These critics included the thinkers Simone de Beauvoir,* noted for her contribution to feminist* theory, and the existentialist* Jean-Paul Sartre,* who had viewed Foucault's previous work *The Order of Things* (1966) as a right-wing attack on Marxism and its related fields. These included phenomenology* (an approach to philosophy that centers on the nature and role of perception in consciousness) and existentialism,[1] a philosophical approach established on the principle that the individual is the foundation of meaning.

The Contemporary Debate

Following in the footsteps of his former teacher, the philosopher Jean Hyppolite,* Foucault rejected the classic interpretation of reason popular during his life. Like Hyppolite, he emphasized the variety of systems of thought and the importance of historical context. The argument about power that Foucault presents in *Discipline and Punish* is key to the book's philosophical claims that reason is historically contingent (that is, based on the ideas of a particular period). According to this view, what may be understood as reasonable, rational, or logical in one age may be considered unreasonable, irrational, or illogical in another. Foucault especially critiques understandings of rationality as something toward which humanity has steadily progressed. He demonstrates the way in which punishment has evolved — from the horrendous spectacle of the gallows to a system that controls and corrects behavior through a variety of forceful methods. In this way, Foucault questions the idea that there has been a steady march of progress toward greater human reason.

Foucault's ideas on the ways in which power is exercised (through the creation of "knowledge" about a person) differs from the materialist interpretation of power in leftist Marxist thought that was so widespread in France at the time. His interpretation of power as "capillary,"[2] meaning that it is always present, even in everyday practices, was opposed to the Marxist econometric* analyses (interpretations of statistical economic data) that saw power as something rooted in material exploitation and the top-down authority of powerful elites.

---

1. Didier Eribon, *Michel Foucault et ses contemporains* (Paris: Fayard, 1994), 155–86.
2. Michel Foucault, *Discipline and Punish: The Birth of the Prison* (Sheridan, NY: Vintage Books, 1979), 198.

MODULE 4
THE AUTHOR'S CONTRIBUTION

KEY POINTS

- Michel Foucault's *Discipline and Punish* sought to trace the history of modern power relations by looking at eighteenth-century prisons and their development into the modern penal system.
- For Foucault, power operates through "power-knowledge,"* which classifies individuals and regulates the movements of their body in time and space through discipline.*
- Unlike the Marxist* thinkers of his time, who focused on how power was based on economic and class position, Foucault looked at the language and mechanisms of power.

Author's Aims

In a series of interviews conducted shortly before his death, Michel Foucault explained that the underlying aim of *Discipline and Punish: The Birth of the Prison* was not to develop a theory of power so much as to understand the history of modern power relations.[1] In the work of the economist and political theorist Karl Marx,* power is exercised by those with economic power; economics* determines who has power. For Foucault, however, power is primary and is not determined by economic position. While in a Marxist political-economic analysis, power is used to repress opposition or to forbid actions, in Foucault's work, power creates: it creates individuals, and social understandings of what those individuals are.

The goal of *Discipline and Punish* is, then, to trace a pattern of power relations as they existed in the eighteenth-century prison. By doing so, Foucault aimed to study the ideas of reason, the body, and the discussions of what was rational and right that developed during that time, and to trace how these ideas have developed up to today. The power relations within the prison help us to understand the makeup of the individual, which in turn helps us to understand how power operates and why it is effective.

In discussing these ideas, Foucault overturned social scientists' ideas of power and rationality* through a critique of Enlightenment* ideas regarding reason and an account of the ways in which knowledge is historically constructed.

> "I am not developing a theory of power. I am working on the history, at a given moment, of the way reflexivity of self upon self is established, and the discourse of truth that is linked to it. When I speak about institutions of confinement in the eighteenth century, I am speaking about power relations as they existed at the time."
>
> —— Michel Foucault, in *Critique and Power: Recasting the Foucault/Habermas Debate*

Approach

Foucault's study of punishment turns on three main, interlinked ideas, which, he argues, form the basis of any regime: power, knowledge, and the body.

Although Foucault has a reputation for continually saying

what power is *not* rather than defining what power *is*, it is worth noting that, for Foucault, power is not understood as something that can be possessed; it is something that creates and operates within social relationships. It is not something that one owns or holds, but rather something one exercises. Power is something that occurs in the tiniest interactions. Power is not the same as conflict or open domination. Power is, rather, productive; it acts through and forms individuals, instead of operating in opposition to their natural or preexisting will.

It is important to remember that *Discipline and Punish* is not concerned with how power operates in relation to specific politics or people. It is concerned with understanding how power operates in modern society and how this type of power came to be.

Foucault describes how the techniques of power depend on an "understanding" of their target. To control something, or someone, one must have "knowledge" of it. "Understanding" and "knowledge" here mean classifying the individual into one of several possible slots. For example, schools and universities keep transcripts of students' grades. In the act of doing so, they are classifying young people as "A," "B," or "C" students and thus creating "knowledge" about the kind of individual each student is. Instead of contesting a "B" grade, and thus the university's classification of them, a student may work harder in order to earn an "A" grade. In this way, the school or university is exercising power over the student. Power and knowledge, then, are deeply interrelated and depend on each other. Foucault's term "power-knowledge"[2] is intended to stress this interconnection.

Finally, Foucault understands the human body as a key target for applying power-knowledge. Institutions create "docile bodies"[3] that self-regulate in order to line up with the norms that are transmitted to them. For example, the soldier walks, talks, and stands in a certain way and through these bodily actions, signals he is lining up with the norms that the army gives him.

For Foucault, power operates through discipline. "Discipline" differs here from its common, everyday use. It refers to a mechanism of power that regulates individuals by acting upon the body in different ways. Discipline may place individuals in different spaces, by assigning them a particular room or cell in a building. It may control them in time, by providing them with a timetable that directs their movements throughout their day. Foucault is careful to make a distinction between discipline on the one hand, and power or punishment on the other. Discipline is not power or punishment as we may understand it. It is, rather, a means by which power operates.

Using these ideas together, Foucault sees the history of punishment as a web of social relations that developed among "power-knowledge"[4] regimes and the human body.

Contribution in Context

In *Discipline and Punish*, Foucault distances himself from structuralism,* phenomenology,* and Marxism — the three schools with which his work was most often associated. His output differed from that of the Marxist scholars of his time in that it did not examine power from an economic point of view, or investigate relations among social classes. The concern, throughout *Discipline and Punish*, is with disciplinary structures, as opposed to economic ones. Similarly, Foucault's genealogy* represented an important break from the fields of phenomenology and structuralism.

Phenomenology and structuralism focus on the structures that allow certain knowledge or beliefs to exist. Foucault's genealogical approach did not concern itself with describing the content of a "knowledge" or belief system. Instead, he was concerned with the mechanisms by which a particular "knowledge" or system of beliefs comes into being. In other words, he is concerned with how a given "truth" is created. Foucault terms this process, and its inner workings, the "politics of the discursive regime"[5] — by which he means that the language we use to represent things is a product and source of power.

1. Michael Kelly et al., *Critique and Power: Recasting the Foucault/Habermas Debate* (Cambridge, Mass.; London: MIT Press, 1994), 129.
2. Michel Foucault, *Discipline and Punish: The Birth of the Prison* (Sheridan, NY: Vintage Books, 1979), 27.
3. Foucault, *Discipline and Punish*, 135.
4. Foucault, *Discipline and Punish*, 27.
5. Michel Foucault, *Power/Knowledge: Selected Interviews and Other Writings, 1972–1977* (New York: Random House Digital, 1980), 118.

SECTION 2
IDEAS

MAIN IDEAS

KEY POINTS

* Foucault's *Discipline and Punish* examines how the rise of the modern prison reflects changes in the exercise of state power over society in general.

* For Foucault, starting in the eighteenth century, states moved from relying on punishment meant to torture and humiliate the body to a more elaborate system of constant control and correction of behavior.

* Foucault refused to follow any particular philosophical category. His writing is considered difficult to read, but he has had a big impact on the social sciences, which have adopted terms he invented, such as "power-knowledge,"* as part of their scholarly vocabulary.

Key Themes

Michel Foucault's *Discipline and Punish: The Birth of the Prison* is concerned with how the evolution of the modern penal system relates to the organization of society at large. Foucault argues that changes in the way states exercised power in the eighteenth century reflect alterations in the structure of society itself, with a shift from a setup of physical and often public punishment to a system of control and correction. We see, he writes, the emergence of prisons tasked with reshaping their subjects; in short, there was a shift from punishment to correction.

This shift had a deep effect on society. Foucault shows this by examining how the correctional methods of the prison bled into society at large, and were used in schools, hospitals, and, eventually, the social sciences themselves. He argues that sociology* and philosophy* as we know them today are rooted in the practices of the first prisons. In the broadest sense, then, *Discipline and Punish*'s main themes are the institutional transformation of power, the rise of a disciplinary regime over society, and the relationship this new form of power has to academic fields including Foucault's own specialty.

This is also a work concerned with the dehumanizing* effects of modern power regimes (that is, the way that modern power regimes strip the individual of their human status, particularly in the light of the assumption that it is less complicated to exercise power on an individual who is not "really human"). Foucault is looking to expose the ways in which we discipline* ourselves, on a daily basis, into being certain kinds of individuals.

Foucault argues that the birth of the modern prison served to create the criminal. With the emergence of the prison, criminals now existed in society in ways that they never had before. First, because criminal offenders were so stigmatized (branded as criminals) and typically released without skills, they often reoffended, and fell into a pattern of career criminality. Second, and more importantly, he argues that the prison produces the criminal by creating a specific social category of the "individual criminal."

This can be called the epistemological production of the criminal. Epistemology* is the study of the origins of knowledge and its limits, and the expression here refers to the systems of knowledge by which the criminal is known — all the ways in which inmates' behavior is tracked, measured, and judged in relation to their original crime and as part of the efforts to reform them. In other words, the penal institution gives rise to the criminal as an identifiable social category — a category of persons known only for the things they have done that society labels as wrong, and the measures being taken to ensure they do not do them again. Foucault argues that putting people in such a category is dehumanizing as it reduces the individual to a list of vital statistics.

In summary, there is a shift from understanding a crime-committing individual as an "individual-who-has-committed-a-crime" to understanding such an individual as a "criminal."

"Basically, I have only one object of historical study, that is the threshold of modernity."
—— Michel Foucault, in *Michel Foucault, entretiens*

Exploring the Ideas

Discipline and Punish opens with the description of two contrasting types of punishment, each of which, Foucault says, represents the penal style of their period. Early forms of punishment sought to shame the body of offenders, he writes; modern forms seek to produce "normality" and conformism.

His first example is a graphic tale of a case of capital punishment — the execution of a man who had attempted to kill the French king in 1757. He was torn limb from limb before a large crowd in a display of ceremonial violence supervised by the state.

Foucault sees this instance as typical of a now-outdated style of punishment, which relied on avenging the crime by humiliating the offender's body.

The second story is of a timetable in a Paris reformatory school eight years later. The reformatory operates on a strict and structured schedule that regulates the lives of its inmates: this regime decides all of the inmates' movements, including when and how much they can eat, sleep, exercise, or wash. In this second scenario, punishment occurs silently, without spectacle or ceremony. The goal is not vengeance, but reform: to reclaim the offenders' souls. Controlling their actions and where they can be ultimately leads to changing their behavior.

For Foucault, this shift toward systems of control that rely on knowledge rather than physical force has deep and wide-reaching implications. The methods and aims of these are symbolic of modern power relations: open violence and coercion* have been replaced by an exercise of power that relies on detailed knowledge of citizens, and long-term intervention intended to correct behavior. As Foucault puts it:"The idea is now to regulate thoroughly and at all times rather than to repress in fits and starts and, by this means, to improve troublesome individuals."[1] For Foucault, this shift from physical punishment to monitoring, measuring, and behavior-correcting marks the beginning of modernity* — the historical period in which we find ourselves today.

Language and Expression

Foucault's arguments are long and complicated and dependent on a very careful examination of aspects that society takes for granted. He is known among scholars for the intricacy and difficulty of his writing style, and his ideas can be hard to follow, even in English translation.

This difficulty may be due, in part, to his obvious efforts to evade being classified. While philosophers generally write in a specific tradition, or anchor their ideas in a specific framework, Foucault sets out, from the beginning of his work, to sketch out a new methodology, refusing to be identified with any one school of thought. Scholars such as the sociologist David Garland have noted that "the literary and rhetorical style in which he formulates his arguments, and the unfamiliarity of the new terms and concepts which litter the text" have earned *Discipline and Punish* a "certain notoriety" among scholars as being both slippery and impenetrable.[2]

This same notoriety, however, has certainly fueled the academic debate around his work. Much of the vocabulary he introduces in the text has since been adopted by philosophers, historians, sociologists, and cultural theorists, and terms such as power-knowledge, "governmentality,"* and "*le regard*"* ("the gaze")[3] have become quite common in discussions about power relations.

---

1. David Garland, "Foucault's *Discipline and Punish* — An Exposition and Critique," *Law & Social Inquiry* 11, no. 4 (1986), 851.

2. Garland, "Foucault's *Discipline and Punish*", 847.

3. Michel Foucault, *Discipline and Punish: The Birth of the Prison* (Sheridan, NY: Vintage Books, 1979), 96.

MODULE 6
SECONDARY IDEAS

KEY POINTS

* Foucault believes modern social structures, including the family, schools, and workplaces, rely on the disciplinary methods of the modern prison. Self-governance by prisoners or citizens who have internalized the rules is crucial.

* Modern society exists, for Foucault, in a "carceral continuum"* in which government pressures people to regulate themselves. This idea influences discussions on education and prison reform.

* An underdeveloped and overlooked aspect of *Discipline and Punish* is Foucault's understanding of "the soul."

Other Ideas

Michel Foucault's *Discipline and Punish: The Birth of the Prison* can also be read as a commentary on the social organization of the family, on the workings of modern educational institutions, and, more generally, on the project of self-governance. He shows the ways in which institutions of social organization such as schools, universities, families, and workplaces have become increasingly subject to the disciplinary techniques of the prison.

Self-governance is crucial to his later works on what he calls "governmentality"* — the methods of regulation that work to get individuals to follow certain behaviors (the "conduct of conduct").[1] In other words, it refers to the ways in which governments seek to produce "ideal" citizens who will follow their rules. "Governmentality" is an important concept, and Foucault develops it in his subsequent texts, including the lectures to the College de France collected in *Security, Territory, Population*[2] and the essay "Governmentality" published in *The Foucault Effect: Studies in Governmentality*.[3]

While less extensively studied than his analysis of panopticism* (the idea that prisoners, or ordinary citizens, can be brought to regulate their own behavior if they know they are being observed), Foucault's understanding of the overlap between modern methods of imprisonment and other social institutions and his concept of "governmentality" are important contributions to the study of power relations (the way in which power is distributed and enforced between different sections of a society).

> *"One must remember that power is not an ensemble of mechanisms of negation, refusal, exclusion. But it produces effectively. It is likely that it produces right down to individuals themselves."*
>
> —— Michel Foucault, in *Michel Foucault, entretiens*

Exploring the Ideas

Foucault, we remember, is concerned with understanding the relationship between carceral* institutions (prisons) and self-governance:"He who is subjected to a field of visibility [being observed], and who knows it," argues Foucault, "assumes responsibility for the constraints of power; he makes them play spontaneously upon himself; he inscribed in himself the power relation in which he simultaneously plays both roles; he becomes the principle of his own subjection."[4]

Studying the history of the modern prison and analyzing the effects of surveillance* on inmates' behavior led Foucault to think about how much other modern institutions depend on self-governance. Modern society relies heavily on getting its citizens used to behaving as if someone might be watching. In this sense, government includes not only formal state structures, but also "problems of self-control, guidance for the family and for children, management of the household, directing the soul, etc."[5]

"Government" operates through decentralized power, and is based on training or pressuring citizens to govern themselves. Placing warning labels on the negative health effects of smoking on cigarette packets is an example of "governmentality." Cigarettes are not banned, and the government does not punish individuals who smoke. And through regulatory measures such as warning labels, norms for behavior are subtly communicated to individuals and they are invited to behave in a certain way. Such a system relies on "instructing" individuals to self-govern. Foucault used this concept to describe advanced liberal democracies (the model on which the majority of Western democracies are based), and argues that in these systems, institutions such as schools and hospitals play a powerful normalizing role.[6] This idea has an influence on contemporary debates around education, prison reform, and public policy.

The other important subtheme in Foucault's work is his understanding of how bodies and people are governed through a process he terms "control of activity."[7] For example, the timetable in a prison or a reform school divides time in a disciplinary fashion, enabling time to penetrate the body completely, and controlling it totally by regimenting all the hours of the day. The timetable is accompanied by a technology of physical efficiency. Mechanisms of surveillance and discipline define each of the relationships between the body and the objects that it encounters. One sees this not just in prisons or reform schools but also in, say, the modern workplace, where one may fear receiving a disapproving glance from a manager or coworker for taking a long lunch, for leaving early, or for doing non-work activities while in the office. The office worker, upon being confronted with the possibility that the manager will see him or her leaving early, may self-regulate such behavior.

Foucault uses these examples to illustrate that a "carceral continuum"*[8] covers the entire pattern of social organization. This continuum is identifiable by a pressing concern with the identification of the anomalous — that which is out of place or not following the rules — and with abnormalities. This framework identifies the most minor infraction with the most major crime, and applies the same disciplinary mechanisms to all.

Overlooked

One aspect of the work has remained largely under-studied: Foucault's understanding of the "soul." Although Foucault himself claims that one of his projects in *Discipline and Punish* is to present a "genealogy* of the modern soul,"[9] the text focuses on the networks of power that shape the soul, not the soul itself.

Foucault's idea of "soul," which refers to the term as it

is used in the Judeo-Christian traditions, is linked to his other arguments on knowledge and power because it pushes aside and replaces the body as the focus of penal reform and surveillance. But critically, Foucault's emphasis on the soul is due to the modern processes of discipline that have structured and created that soul. Without discipline, surveillance, and the human sciences (including the mechanisms of observation and examination central to criminology* — the study of matters related to crime and criminal behavior — and the sciences of psychology* and psychiatry*), the normal soul as such would not exist.

"This real, non-corporal soul is not a substance; it is the element in which are articulated the effects of a certain type of power and the reference of a certain type of knowledge,"[10] Foucault writes. In contrast to the traditional Judeo-Christian conception of the body as the prison of the soul, he takes the soul to be the "prison of the body."[11]

This concept has been used to anchor others' investigations of modern identity. For example, the influential social theorist Nikolas Rose* uses it as a starting point in his book *Governing the Soul*. The book first traces the development of some of the more important ideas in psychological practice in the twentieth century, and then attempts analytically to stretch psychology into economic life in much the way that Foucault does: by examining the way that social experts shape our lives and self-understandings. Such forces are an attempt to line up political and social goals of governance with individual-level desires, pleasures, and feelings; it is a meeting of institutional goals through self-fulfillment.[12]

1. Graham Burchell et al., eds., *The Foucault Effect: Studies in Governmentality* (Chicago, IL: University of Chicago Press, 1991), 2.

2. Michel Foucault, *Security, Territory, Population, Lectures to the Collège de France, 1977–78* (London and New York: Palgrave MacMillan, 2007).

3. Burchell et al., *The Foucault Effect*.

4. Michel Foucault, *Discipline and Punish: The Birth of the Prison* (Sheridan, NY: Vintage Books, 1979), 202–3.

5. Thomas Lemke, "'The Birth of Bio-politics': Michel Foucault's Lecture at the Collège De France on Neo-liberal Governmentality," *Economy and Society* 30, no. 2 (2001), 2.

6. Michel Foucault, "Governmentality," in *The Essential Foucault*, ed. Paul Rabinow and Nikolas Rose (New York and London: The New Press, 2003), 102–3.

7. Foucault, *Discipline and Punish*, 149.

8. Foucault, *Discipline and Punish*, 293.

9. Foucault, *Discipline and Punish*, 23.

10. Foucault, *Discipline and Punish*, 29.

11. Foucault, *Discipline and Punish*, 29.

12. Nikolas Rose, *Governing the Soul: The Shaping of the Private Self* (Florence, KY: Taylor & Francis/Routledge, 1990), 258.

MODULE 7
ACHIEVEMENT

KEY POINTS

* Michel Foucault's *Discipline and Punish* radically redefined the way sociologists and philosophers thought about modern power relations and their role in shaping society, culture, and identity.

* Its reception was influenced by its sociopolitical context: the radical French politics of the 1960s and 1970s, which his work reflected.

* Despite its positive reception, *Discipline and Punish* has not been without its critics. The sociologist Zygmunt Bauman,* for example, says today that most people are seduced, and not coerced, into following society's norms.

Assessing the Argument

Michel Foucault's *Discipline and Punish* attempted to illustrate the evolution of the power of modern institutions through the history of the modern penal system. By tracing the story of the modern prison, and showing the shift from public displays of punishment to systems of correction through means of observation and control, Foucault demonstrated the relationship between power, knowledge, the individual, and conformity. The key difference between ancient or feudal and modern styles of punishment is that modern institutions seek to reform the offender. Through monitoring and control, the system is able to mold a person to its liking, ensuring he or she conforms to a particular set of criteria. A system that gathers knowledge about its subjects can gain insight into their behavior and the reasons behind it, and make regulations to encourage individuals to self-regulate.

Foucault demonstrates the wide-reaching implications of this new form of power. The workings of our schools, hospitals, factories, and offices all rely on the same principles of surveillance* and knowledge-gathering that constitute the modern prison. Moreover, the social sciences and their practices of data-gathering, subject-monitoring, and condition-diagnosing are rooted in these same ideas: academic thought in the sciences and humanities owes its existence to the principles of modern disciplinary regimes.

> "This book is intended as a correlative history of the modern soul and of a new power to judge."
> ——Michel Foucault, *Discipline and Punish: The Birth of the Prison*

Achievement in Context

Foucault's work radically redefined the fields of philosophy* and sociology,* and particularly influenced the sociology of punishment,* a subdiscipline of sociology that explores the relationship between punishment and society. Until the publication of *Discipline and Punish*, this subdiscipline had relied heavily on the ideas of Emile Durkheim,*[1] the late nineteenth-and early twentieth-century founder of sociology, who emphasized the role of social institutions and social structure in organizing social life. Until the 1970s, the study of punishment remained largely the remit of criminologists* (scholars of crime and criminals) and penologists* (scholars of punishment and prisons), who approached it as a technical issue rather than a sociological one. In other words, they focused on how to punish more effectively, instead of focusing on the history and implications of the forms of punishment imposed by institutions.

In this sense, Foucault's work both helped to redefine the scope of intellectual thought in his field and developed a new approach for understanding power relations across multiple disciplines.

Beyond its specific contributions, the book's critical reception was also clearly helped by the sociopolitical climate of the time. The radical politics of the late 1960s and early 1970s, which included the student protests in Paris in May 1968,* opposition to the Vietnam War,* and anti-colonialist sentiment among French intellectuals, made Foucault's ideas intensely relevant for his readers at the time. His understanding of the way power and knowledge work together to create conformity found a ready audience in intellectuals unhappy with the state of the French education system, the seeming elitism of academia, and the country's role in oppressing its colonies.*

Limitations

First published in 1975, *Discipline and Punish* spoke to many of the sociopolitical concerns of its time, and it is often regarded as reflecting French leftist sentiment of the 1960s and 1970s. What makes it a key work across the humanities and social sciences, however, is that it can be applied beyond that period, and beyond the disciplines of sociology, philosophy, and history from which it emerged. Foucault's historical approach, which traces the story of punishment from the Middle Ages to modernity* (the modern period), and which identifies the first instances of modern discipline,* is specifically designed to provide a way of understanding power in various contexts, and across various historical periods.

In the text, Foucault's concern is not with the mechanisms of power in France in the 1960s and 1970s, but rather with the workings of modern power in the abstract: how power works in any modern context. His central ideas — the role of surveillance, control, and knowledge-gathering — can be applied to a variety of different settings, and are not limited to specific forms of governance. So, for example, his ideas remain acutely relevant to the concerns of twenty-first-century readers living in a neoliberal* globalized* economy, since this system, too, relies on surveillance mechanisms, data-gathering, and monitoring of its citizens. ("Neoliberal" here refers to the current economic orthodoxy that the route to economic growth lies through unregulated free trade, privatization, and the smallest amount of governmental intervention possible, and so on; "globalization" refers to the increasing convergence of the world's economies and cultures.) In fact, in light of technological developments such as the Internet and closed-circuit television (CCTV)* — which did not exist in Foucault's time — one might even argue that the ideas expressed in *Discipline and Punish* are more relevant now than when the book was first published. This is one reason why it is regularly used today in scholarship on digital culture.*

Despite *Discipline and Punish*'s positive reception, it has not been immune to criticism. The leading sociologist Zygmunt Bauman, for example, argues that disciplinary society marked a certain moment in modernity in which large layers of the population needed to be regulated efficiently. This was the age of the army and the factory. Disciplinary society, however, as Foucault formulated it, is less relevant in post-modern society. For Bauman, "The great majority of people ... are today integrated through seduction rather than policing, advertising rather than indoctrinating, need-creation rather than normative regulation."[2] In other words, we are seduced, rather than monitored into being certain kinds of subjects. We desire to, for example, be fit and healthy individuals not because we are being watched by the authorities, but because advertising seduces us into wanting to be fit and healthy.

---

1. See: Emile Durkheim and Lewis A. Coser, *The Division of Labor in Society* (New York, NY: Free Press, 1997).

2. Zygmunt Bauman, "On Postmodern Uses of Sex," *Theory, Culture & Society* 15, no. 3 (1998): 23.

PLACE IN THE AUTHOR'S WORK

KEY POINTS

- Michel Foucault explored the relationship between history, normality, and abnormality throughout his career. He was particularly concerned with how institutions impose certain norms of behavior by branding people who step out of line.

- *Discipline and Punish* was among Foucault's last published works, and is viewed by scholars as marking the beginning of his "genealogical"* phase, which they distinguish from his earlier "archaeological"* phase.

- The text has remained relevant through the changing relationships between the state and its citizens, first under the welfare state* (in which the government ensures a degree of security for its citizens) and then neoliberalism* (in which the government intervenes as little as possible in the economic lives of its citizens).

Positioning

Discipline and Punish: The Birth of the Prison is a product of Michel Foucault's long concern with the role played by labels such as "madness" or "criminality" in creating and maintaining structures of power, and in the ways norms for behavior are communicated to citizens. In *Madness and Civilization* (1961), for example, Foucault distinguishes mental illness from "madness." He argues that the latter is a social construct used by institutions to brand people who deviate from the norm. As with his later publications, his 1961 book takes a historical approach, using the history of medicine to critique modern assumptions about mental health and so-called "normality."

Foucault's later works, *The Birth of the Clinic* (1963) and *The Order of Things* (1966), extended some of these ideas. *The Birth of the Clinic* traced the history of medicine from the late eighteenth and early nineteenth centuries, a period of huge transformation and radical development of new technologies. *The Order of Things* examined science as a whole, arguing that throughout history, scientific discourse has had to accept certain assumptions as the "truth" — but that these so-called facts have differed from era to era.

Foucault began writing *Discipline and Punish* in the late 1960s, and the work represents a later stage in his intellectual life. Foucault himself often referred to the text as his "first book"[1] because he thought it the one that most fully and faithfully developed his thought. It also served as a bridge to his later ideas; for example, while Foucault first mentioned "governmentality"* in *Discipline and Punish*, he developed it more fully in later works.

> "If you are not like everybody else, then you are abnormal; if you are abnormal, then you are sick. These three categories, not being like everybody else, not being normal and being sick are in fact very different but they have been reduced to the same thing."
> —— Michel Foucault, in *Michel Foucault, entretiens*

Integration

Although *Discipline and Punish* brings together concepts that concerned Foucault throughout his life — such as history,* power-knowledge,* normalization,* and self-governance* — it also marks a departure from his previous work. The study is his first effort to apply a "genealogical" approach to history, as opposed to the "archaeological" approach of his previous historical projects. These methods differ in several important ways.

An archaeological approach is based on the idea that systems of thought are regulated by subconscious mechanisms within individuals. It seeks to place and explore systems of knowledge in relation to the conditions from which they emerged. As such, it can be thought of as an exploration of possibilities: of the creation of the potentials that shape thought. Unlike both the philosophical approach of phenomenology* and traditional history, an archaeological method does not draw on expressions of individual psychology*; rather, it looks at how thoughts, ideas, and discursive* practices — culturally and historically specific rules for producing knowledge — are formed. That said, archaeology can compare only different discursive practices and ways of knowing that operate at different times or in different contexts. It is not equipped to articulate the *causes* of changes in thinking or the variations in discursive practice.

Foucault's concept of genealogy was intended to remedy this theoretical and methodological shortcoming. The term itself was a reference to Friedrich Nietzsche's* "genealogy of morals." By using a genealogical approach, *Discipline and Punish* aimed to demonstrate that any given system of knowledge or thinking was the result of historically contingent* events — the result of the history that came before it. In other words, genealogy is a way of explaining the present by placing it in relation to the past. Foucault's genealogical approach is concerned with the mechanisms by which a particular science or system of beliefs comes into being — which is also to say, how a given "truth" is created. Foucault terms this process, and its inner workings, the "politics of the discursive regime."[2] In broader terms, then, the text extends Foucault's life-long concern with questioning the very discourse of philosophy* itself, and challenging what he saw as its uncritical tendencies.

Significance

Foucault's *Discipline and Punish* turned out to be more useful than perhaps even he had expected, as its ideas have remained valid even as the socioeconomic landscape of the West has changed. Foucault worked on the text in the 1960s and through the 1970s, just as the Bretton Woods* international monetary system was abandoned and, along with it, the financial philosophies that provided the theoretical foundation for the welfare state.

Bretton Woods was a system of monetary management that regulated commercial and financial relationships among the major industrial economies from just after World War II until the early 1970s. The system allowed governments to play a greater role in international and national power relations than that which we experience today. The "welfare state" refers to the many government-funded institutions and programs that provide care to a state's citizens — including health care, social security, and other social benefits.

Under these two regimes, the dynamics described by Foucault would occur between government officials and citizens: between a social worker and a youth offender, for example, or between a psychologist and a patient, or a parole officer and his or her charge. Foucault's primary concern was with the disciplinary mechanisms used by these state initiatives. The point underlying his critique was that specialties such as social work and health care, which we assume to be progressive, apolitical, and benevolent, are, in fact, involved with the subjugation,* surveillance,* and control of citizens.

These same ideas, however, turned out also to be widely valid under neoliberalism, the economic regime that took the place of Bretton Woods, and which exists to this day. Neoliberalism is a set of economic policies that promotes economic liberalization, free trade, open markets, privatization, deregulation, and strengthening of the role of the private sector, and it has proven to raise similar concerns about surveillance, individual privacy, and choice as the system it replaced.[3] In this sense, then, *Discipline and Punish* has been effective, remaining relevant to the concerns of scholars and critics in the globalized* world today.

It is also thanks to this timelessness and universality that the text has had such a far-reaching influence. Its examination of the relationship between power, knowledge, surveillance, and the individual are relevant to contemporary discussions about privacy, data-collection, and the spread and use of information in the digital age. As well as radically redefining the fields of sociology and philosophy, *Discipline and Punish* has since proven a useful document for understanding power relations today.

---

1. James Miller, *The Passion of Michel Foucault* (Cambridge, MA: Harvard University Press, 1993).

2. Michel Foucault, *Power/Knowledge: Selected Interviews and Other Writings, 1972–1977* (New York: Random House Digital, 1980), 118.

3. Nancy Fraser, "From Discipline to Flexibilization? Rereading Foucault in the Shadow of Globalization," *Constellations* 10, no. 2 (2003): 160–71.

SECTION 3
IMPACT

THE FIRST RESPONSES

KEY POINTS

* Michel Foucault's *Discipline and Punish* was met with criticism after its publication, most famously from the social scientist and philosopher Jürgen Habermas,* who took issue with Foucault's critique of the thinking of the period of European intellectual history known as the Enlightenment* and his claim that reason itself is socially constructed.

* Foucault and Habermas engaged in a debate over these issues throughout the last years of Foucault's life.

* *Discipline and Punish* has also been criticized for being an inaccurate representation of how power works in prisons.

Criticism

Michel Foucault's *Discipline and Punish* inspired intense criticism when it was first published. The most famous came from Jürgen Habermas, a highly regarded social scientist and philosopher. Habermas's critique and the debate that followed, which is known among scholars as the "Foucault-Habermas debate," engaged both thinkers for a number of years, and spanned a number of their works.

Habermas has been the strongest contemporary defender of the Enlightenment's faith in reason, approaching power from a radically different point of view: from what he terms "communicative rationality"* and "discourse* ethics."[1] By this he means, roughly, that reason is possible and is the outcome of successful communication. While Foucault argues that there is no fixed human character, and that reason is historically produced and contingent* (that is, its historical context is crucial), Habermas contends that there is a fixed human character, and that reason can solve human dilemmas.

Second, Habermas argues that only practices which produce free communication can generate legitimate social organization. The whole idea of this theory is deeply at odds with Foucault, as it differs from Foucault's claim that social interaction itself is always structured and constrained by power. Further, he argues that Foucault wrongly reduces all culture and politics to violence, and social life to a series of power interactions.

Habermas and Foucault were also in conflict in their methodological approach. Habermas accuses Foucault of being "utterly unsociological," which is to say that Foucault did not follow the scientific method.[2] Other critics, such as the political philosopher Nancy Fraser,* have criticized Foucault's work on similar lines; Foucault, Fraser argues, encourages us to criticize modern society while telling us that criticism is pointless as we cannot escape from power.

> *"The constant division between the normal and the abnormal, to which every individual is subjected, brings us back to our own time, by applying the binary branding and exile of the leper to quite different objects; the existence of the whole set of techniques and institutions for measuring, supervising and correcting the abnormal brings into play the disciplinary mechanisms to which the fear of the plague gave rise."*
>
> —— Michel Foucault, *Discipline and Punish: The Birth of the Prison*

Responses

One of Foucault's most famous responses to Habermas appears in the essay "What is Enlightenment?" written toward the end of his life. In this essay, Foucault argues that modernity* and the Enlightenment are attitudes, rather than periods in history. The goal is not to find universal human values or characteristics but, rather, to understand how it is we came to be. Further, instead of searching for a basic humanity, we should instead consider the kind of selves we want to be.

Foucault insists that his perspective on truth and power contains more nuances than Habermas supposes. Instead of being a critique of the possibility of reason or rationality,* Foucault saw his work as a study of the practice of contrasting rationality with irrationality. For Foucault, his whole project seeks to demonstrate that the use of those two categories themselves — and their placement in a hierarchy — is too simplistic.

Foucault also argues against Habermas's view that truth and reason are absolute — which is to say, that one is either in truth or in error. For Habermas, rationality is truth. There is only one truth, and there exists a precise distinction between truth and untruth. But Foucault considers this sort of dichotomy to be a form of "intellectual blackmail."[3] Reason, he argues, is deeply subjective: it is socially constructed (that is, a product of particular social circumstances), and dependent on historical and cultural contexts. For Foucault, "reason is self-created, which is why I have tried to analyze forms of rationality: different foundations, different creations, different modifications in which rationalities engender one another, oppose and pursue one another."[4] The process by which we come to assume certain things to be true, for him, is most worthy of our study: Foucault is interested in how particular systems of knowledge come about, and how those systems undermine or affirm existing power dynamics. The critique of knowledge itself — including our understanding of truth, and our processes of reflection — is a crucial part of his project.

Conflict and Consensus

In the four decades since its publication, aspects of *Discipline and Punish* have continued to attract controversy. For example, the political psychologist C. Fred Alford* has criticized what he sees as Foucault's methodological failings.[5] Drawing on his own ethnographic experience studying prisons in the United States, Alford argues that the disciplinary practices upon which Foucault develops his argument are, in fact, absent from modern prisons, and suggests that the opposite principle is visible. For Alford, discipline in prisons occurs through the control of entrances and exits rather than through the constant possibility of surveillance* — supervising entrances and exits renders surveillance irrelevant. Prison authorities don't watch prisoners, he argues, because their power is already shown in their ability to direct comings and goings. They have the power not to care enough to look. Alford claims that Foucault founds his arguments on theories and ideas about prisons that do not relate to the historical reality. For instance, the theoretical prison inside which inmates could never be certain they were unobserved, the Panopticon,* was never constructed — but writing as if these prison reforms took place, Foucault mistakes ideological claims for practice. This, further, confuses his understanding of power.

Voicing a relatively common critique of Foucault, Alford further criticizes him for writing as if the new disciplinary practices were completely different from older or more "traditional" modes of power. Alford argues, against Foucault, that disciplinary practices are indeed exercised by all rulers and authorities.

---

1. Jürgen Habermas, *The Theory of Communicative Action, Vol. 1: Reason and the Rationalization of Society* (Boston, MA: Beacon Press, 1984).

2. Didier Eribon, *Michel Foucault et ses contemporains* (Paris: Fayard, 1994), 155–86.

3. Michel Foucault, "What Is Enlightenment?," in *The Foucault Effect: Studies in Governmentality*, ed. Graham Burchell et al. (Chicago, IL: University of Chicago Press, 1991), 42.

4. Quoted in Michael Kelly et al., *Critique and Power: Recasting the Foucault/Habermas Debate* (Cambridge, Mass.; London: MIT Press, 1994), 119.

5. C. Fred Alford, "What Would It Matter if Everything Foucault Said About Prison Were Wrong? *Discipline and Punish* After Twenty Years," *Theory and Society* 29, no. 1 (2000): 125–46.

MODULE 10
THE EVOLVING DEBATE

KEY POINTS

• While scholars in a variety of disciplines have taken up the ideas in *Discipline and Punish*, even the book's basic assumptions have attracted sharp criticism.

• The text led to the development of the sociology of punishment* (the analysis of why and how we punish,) and has helped shape the vocabulary of numerous subfields of sociology, including organizational sociology* (a branch of sociology that looks at organizations) and sociology of law.*

• Scholars have found concepts of "power-knowledge"* and "discipline"* particularly useful.

Uses and Problems

Michel Foucault's *Discipline and Punish* remains a key text for sociologists and philosophers, theorists, social scientists, and scholars of the humanities. New writers following Foucault's lead have used the concepts found in *Discipline and Punish*, such as discipline and panopticism,* to chart the overlapping of power and the modern individual. Scholars have used Foucault's theoretical insights as a framework to examine a variety of issues that he could not have predicted, such as thinking about obesity[1] or human resource management.*[2]

That said, *Discipline and Punish* has not been free from criticism. In lectures he gave a few years after the publication of the text, collected in the book *Security, Territory, Population*, Foucault himself criticized the earlier work's overemphasis on discipline as a restriction on individual freedom. In a refinement of his earlier thought, Foucault argued that we must conceive of power as something that thinks "of men's freedom, of what they want to do, of what they have an interest in doing, and of what they think about doing" and as "a regulation that can only be carried out through and by reliance on the freedom of each."[3] The social theorist Nikolas Rose* has developed these ideas further in *Powers of Freedom: Reframing Political Thought*,[4] which extends this argument in order to consider the ways in which individual freedom becomes a task of modern governance.

Other scholars have attempted to update his account of panopticism. The Norwegian sociologist Thomas Mathiesen, for instance, has argued that power lies not in the model of the Panopticon,* in which the few watch the many, but in what he calls the "Synopticon," in which the many watch the few. He argues that we live not in a disciplinary society but in a viewer society. He uses as evidence the rise of celebrity culture and the mass media, in

> "The human body was entering a machinery of power that explores it, breaks it down and rearranges it. A 'political anatomy', which was also a 'mechanics of power', was being born; it defined how one may have a hold over others' bodies, not only so that they may do what one wishes, but so that they may operate as one wishes, with the techniques, the speed and the efficiency that one determines. Thus discipline produces subjected and practiced bodies, 'docile' bodies."
>
> —— Michel Foucault, *Discipline and Punish: The Birth of the Prison*

which the general public — the "many" — model their behavior by watching the actions of "the few" — be they celebrities, politicians, or other public figures in current culture.[5]

Schools of Thought

From the late 1970s, a new variation of studies of carceral* institutions (places in which people are incarcerated) has begun to emerge, most of which now focus on the role of prisons in creating and maintaining a social order rather than on punishment itself. These new studies, broadly referred to as the sociology of punishment, rely on concepts found in Foucault's texts, including state control and the processes by which individuals are created as social subjects.

Foucault's work can be credited for this development in several ways. First, according to one scholar, Foucault "demonstrated to a wide audience of historians and social theorists the far-reaching sociological significance of punishment and the kinds of insights which might be gained from a close examination of its practices."[6] It also created an important set of tools for understanding state control. Foucault's ideas about penalty and criminal regulation have since been adopted and refined within the subdiscipline. These changes are important, and can be seen in the very language with which sociologists now discuss law, penalty, control, and state power:"Discipline," "surveillance,"* "power-knowledge," and "normalization"* are all routine parts of contemporary sociological vocabulary.

Sociologists of the law have followed suit,[7] attempting to create frameworks that understand law as governance and discipline; some scholars have even constructed what they term a "Foucauldian theory of the law," emphasizing the ways by which the law should be understood as a form of governance.

In Current Scholarship

The influence of *Discipline and Punish* has spread widely throughout the social sciences and humanities. Recently, the unlikely subfields of organizational sociology* and management have absorbed some of the key insights of the text — and the body of Foucault's work in general — with unusual applications to other areas of social science and social life. For example, the American social geographer and food scholar Julie Guthman uses the concept of "power-knowledge" to discuss how ideas of health interact with access to food to produce dramatically unequal societies.[8] The British management economist Barbara Townley,* meanwhile, argues that the practice of human resource management can be best understood as a discursive regime that renders employees governable through practices of subject-making similar to techniques deployed in the Panopticon.[9] Likewise, the organizational theorist Gibson Burrell's work looks at how organizations are mechanisms of surveillance and discipline.*[10]

With respect to organizational sociology and administrative science* in particular, *Discipline and Punish* remains a highly original contribution. Organizational sociology relies, in no small part, on concepts of rationality* and efficiency, and benefits dramatically (though often uncomfortably) from a Foucault-style analysis that questions the nature of power, governance, and the individuals involved.

1. Julie Guthman and Melanie DuPuis, "Embodying Neoliberalism: Economy, Culture, and the Politics of Fat," *Environment and Planning D: Society and Space* 24, no. 3 (2006): 427–48.

2. Barbara Townley, "Foucault, Power/Knowledge, and Its Relevance for Human Resource Management," *The Academy of Management Review* 18, no. 3 (July 1993): 518–45.

3. Michel Foucault, *Security, Territory, Population, Lectures to the Collège de France 1977–1978* (London and New York: Palgrave Macmillan, 2007): 49.

4. Nikolas Rose, *Powers of Freedom: Reframing Political Thought* (Cambridge: Cambridge University Press, 1999).

5. Thomas Mathiesen, "The Viewer Society: Foucault's Panopticon Revisited," *Theoretical Criminology* 1, no. 2 (1997).

6. David Garland, "Frameworks of Inquiry in the Sociology of Punishment," *The British Journal of Sociology* 41, no. 1 (March 1990): 2.

7. See: Alan Hunt and Gary Wickham, *Foucault and Law: Towards a Sociology of Law as Governance* (Boulder, CO and London: Pluto Press, 1994).

8. Guthman and DuPuis, "Embodying Neoliberalism," 427–48.

9. Townley, "Foucault, Power/Knowledge," 518–45.

10. Gibson Burrell, "Modernism, Post Modernism and Organizational Analysis 2: The Contribution of Michel Foucault," *Organization Studies* 9, no. 2 (April 1988): 221–35.

IMPACT AND INFLUENCE TODAY

KEY POINTS

* Michel Foucault's *Discipline and Punish* has become a core work both in its original fields of sociology* and history,* and in other humanities and social science disciplines.

* Foucault's ideas have been used to examine issues as varied as obesity, sexuality, ethics, and the epistemological* status of the state — that is, the place of the state according to theories of what can be known and how we come to know it.

* The Habermas-Foucault debates have continued, even after Foucault's death, as scholars continue to discuss the contrasting views of reason.

Position

Michel Foucault's *Discipline and Punish* remains a central text in diverse fields, especially in history, anthropology,* and sociology. Although there are variations, sociologists who follow Foucault focus largely on power, discourse* (for Foucault, a way of speaking that arises from the influence of history and power, but elsewhere a term signifying, roughly, the exchange of ideas that defines how something is understood), the body, and the creation of the individual. These are all themes that Foucault examined closely.

The organizational sociologist* Nancy Fraser,*[1] the political sociologist Barbara Townley,* and the development scholar James Ferguson[2] all use the concept of "discourse" in their work. Nancy Fraser in particular has written provocatively about how Foucault's thinking on discipline,* written in the 1950s and 1960s while governmental intervention in the economy and investment in the welfare state* formed economic orthodoxy, can be applied to the more globalized* neoliberal* state that exists today, where markets are left to their own devices and ensuring social justice and welfare is less of a priority. She explores his ideas of how the state and the market create discourses around self-governance. Similarly, sociologists of punishment and crime such as David Garland,[3] Joachim Savelsberg,[4] and John Braithwaite[5] have been influenced by Foucault's understanding of punishment as a form of social control.

A number of scholars have absorbed Foucault's work on the human body, adapting it for theoretical emphasis on matters as diverse as obesity,[6] feminist studies,[*7] queer theory[*8] (scholarly inquiry into gender and identity often conducted with a view to challenge traditional understandings of each), and the development of anatomical science.[9] These thinkers take their cue from Foucault's understanding of the body as the site of discipline and the target of disciplining technologies in order to think about how minority or marginalized groups are made to conform.

Meanwhile, theorists of the state such as Robert Jessop[10] and Thomas Lemke[11] have applied Foucault's thinking to an analysis of government, including the centrality of "power-knowledge"[*12] and discursive practices (the production and organization of knowledge) within the state. For Jessop and Lemke, Foucault provides the basis for a theoretical understanding of technologies of governance. Foucault allows us, they say, to shift from seeing the state as a singular entity that governs from above, to seeing governance as being made up of the actions and practices of a varied set of actors. An example of the kind of shift of which they are talking could be government partnerships with non-profit organizations or charities that provide, for example, support for substance abusers or those who engage in other forms of deviant behavior. These practices often work on the basis of discipline — through individuals' self-regulation.

> *"Is it surprising that prisons resemble factories, schools, barracks, and hospitals, which all resemble prisons?"*
> —— Michel Foucault, *Discipline and Punish: The Birth of the Prison*

Interaction

Although *Discipline and Punish* studies history, sociology, criminology,* and cultural theory*, it belongs to all and none of these genres, making it hard to place it in any one subdiscipline or tradition. For this reason, Foucault's theorizing has some of the broadest implications of any current thinker — which is why it has been interpreted across a number of different academic fields. For example, the anthropologist James Faubion has employed Foucault's thinking on social institutions in his study of ethics;[13] the classicist David Larmour has used his work in thinking on sexuality and antiquity;[14] and the historian Vazira Zamindar writes on boundaries and citizens using ideas of the creation of individual identities and discipline found in Foucault's work.[15]

What these very different Foucauldian scholars share is a tendency to seek out institutional histories, to identify social control, and to adopt methods that mimic Foucault's genealogy.* Foucault lends himself to such projects, since he provides a widely applicable method via which scholars can examine the flow of power and knowledge in any arena or historical context.

The Continuing Debate

Foucault and the sociologist Jürgen Habermas* had only just overcome the bitterness that had previously characterized their debate when Foucault died in 1984. So it fell to Foucault's followers to continue the discourse. The debate takes up the very nature of rationality* and, by extension, the possibility for human emancipation* (that is, liberation, as if from slavery). Scholars of reason and critical theory retain an active engagement in the Foucault-Habermas debate, as it speaks to a basic principle of social theory: whether or not human societies are by nature prone to conflict.

Scholars who follow Foucault have, by and large, dismissed Habermas's critique of Foucault's supposed relativism (that is, his supposed belief that there are no absolutes in certain matters) as invalid because it tends to "presuppose what it seeks to show."[16] Others have continued to argue that the Habermasian analysis is based on a misunderstanding of the substance of Foucault's work. These scholars include the likes of Michael Kelly, who defends Foucault, arguing that Habermas has misunderstood the

145

ideas of both disciplinary power and local critique. Kelly says that although Foucault criticizes the dominant forms of rationality that have been present since the Enlightenment,* he at no time argues that reason itself is worthless.[17] And in their 1999 book, *Foucault contra Habermas: Recasting the Dialogue Between Genealogy and Critical Theory*, the sociologists Samantha Ashenden and David Owen attempt to breathe new life into the debate by providing a "Foucauldian rejoinder" to later Habermasian critiques.

1. Nancy Fraser, "From Discipline to Flexibilization? Rereading Foucault in the Shadow of Globalization," *Constellations* 10, no. 2 (2003).

2. James Ferguson, *The Anti-politics Machine: Development, Depoliticization, and Bureaucratic Power in Lesotho* (Minneapolis: University of Minnesota Press, 1994).

3. See: David Garland, "Frameworks of Inquiry in the Sociology of Punishment," *The British Journal of Sociology* 41, no. 1 (March 1990).

4. Joachim J. Savelsberg, "Knowledge, Domination, and Criminal Punishment," *American Journal of Sociology* 99, no. 4 (January 1994): 911–43.

5. John Braithwaite, "What's Wrong with the Sociology of Punishment?" *Theoretical Criminology* 7, no. 1 (February 2003): 5–28.

6. Julie Guthman and Melanie DuPuis, "Embodying Neoliberalism: Economy, Culture, and the Politics of Fat," *Environment and Planning D: Society and Space* 24, no. 3 (2006): 427–48.

7. Jana Sawicki, *Disciplining Foucault: Feminism, Power, and the Body* (London: Routledge, 1991); Susan Hekman, ed., *Feminist Interpretations of Michel Foucault* (University Park, PA: Pennsylvania State University Press, 1996).

8. David Halperin, *Saint Foucault: Towards a Gay Hagiography* (Oxford and New York: Oxford University Press, 1997).

9. Jan C. Rupp, "Michel Foucault, Body Politics and the Rise and Expansion of Modern Anatomy," *Journal of Historical Sociology* 5, no. 1 (1992): 31–60.

10. Bob Jessop, "From Micro-powers to Governmentality: Foucault's Work on Statehood, State Formation, Statecraft and State Power," *Political Geography* 26, no. 1 (January 2007): 34–40.

11. Thomas Lemke, "An Indigestible Meal? Foucault, Governmentality and State Theory," *Distinktion:*

Scandinavian Journal of Social Theory 8, no. 2 (2007): 43–64.

12. Michel Foucault. *Discipline and Punish: The Birth of the Prison* (Sheridan, NY: Vintage Books, 1979): 27.

13. James D. Faubion, "Toward an Anthropology of Ethics: Foucault and the Pedagogies of Autopoiesis," *Representations* 74, no. 1 (Spring 2001): 83–104.

14. David H. J. Larmour et al., *Rethinking Sexuality: Foucault and Classical Antiquity* (Princeton, NJ: Princeton University Press, 1997).

15. Vazira Fazila-Yacoobali Zamindar, *The Long Partition and the Making of Modern South Asia: Refugees, Boundaries, Histories* (New York, NY: Columbia University Press, 2007).

16. Samantha Ashenden and David Owen, *Foucault Contra Habermas: Recasting the Dialogue Between Genealogy and Critical Theory* (Thousand Oaks, CA; London: SAGE, 1999).

17. Michael Kelly et al., *Critique and Power: Recasting the Foucault/Habermas Debate* (Cambridge, MA; London: MIT Press, 1994), 372.

WHERE NEXT?

KEY POINTS

• Michel Foucault's *Discipline and Punish* remains an important text for humanities and social science scholars interested in modern power relations.

• The work has wide applications in contemporary discussions about digital surveillance* mechanisms and individual privacy. It has also had a marked influence in the sociology of health and illness.

• Foucault's study is timeless, as it examines the techniques and mechanisms used in power relations rather than explicitly attacking a specific group or institution's exercise of power.

Potential

Michel Foucault's *Discipline and Punish* remains a key text for scholars in the humanities and social sciences, and has wide applications beyond sociology,* in fields as diverse as international relations,* digital culture studies,* law, literary studies,* feminist* criticism, queer theory,* and cultural theory.* This in itself is something of a paradox, given that so much of Foucault's work was written as a critique of academic discourse, and was in opposition to the fields that have since absorbed him.

The way his work can be applied to the discussion of technologies that did not exist in his lifetime is a further tribute to its timelessness. It is remarkable to think that when Foucault wrote the words "visibility is a trap,"[1] CCTV* cameras and the

Internet did not yet exist. In this sense, he anticipated with uncanny foresight some key aspects of the power relations of the world in which we live today. Indeed, Foucault's work has gained renewed attention in the past decade in scholarly and public debates about individual privacy in the digital age, and in discussions about power in neoliberal* globalized* economies. For example, the anti-capitalist scholars Michael Hardt* and Antonio Negri* argue that Foucault's work has "prepared the terrain for [...] an investigation of the material functioning of imperial rule."[2] Still, other parts of the leftist movement see Foucault's insistence that there is no absolute right and wrong as a curse, calling him a "crucial source of the malaise affecting the rest of the left — the gutless relativism which prevents [action]."[3]

His work is widely cited in discussions about digital surveillance, including, most recently, David M. Berry's *Critical Theory and the Digital* (2014),[4] and the fourth edition of Cynthia Weber's key guide to contemporary international relations* theory. Weber concisely explains the lasting relevance of Foucault's ideas in the digital age and shows the extent to which his ideas anticipated Edward Snowden's* disclosures of US government surveillance.[5] And in *Crime, Justice and the Media* (2009), Ian Marsh and Gaynor Melville examine the logical extension of these ideas, addressing the issue of how the circulation of certain types of information — including biased accounts of events — helps strengthen and maintain social control.[6] Finally, David Lyon's *Theorizing Surveillance* (2006) uses Foucault's ideas as a starting point for conceptualizing the role of surveillance in contemporary society. Each contributor in the collection examines surveillance from a Foucauldian, or anti-Foucauldian, point of view.[7]

> "Visibility is a trap."
>
> —— Michel Foucault, *Discipline and Punish:*
> *The Birth of the Prison*

Future Directions

Foucault's mark in the social sciences has been exceptionally powerful in the field of the sociology of health and illness. This is particularly noteworthy given that the sociology of health and illness has traditionally understood the body as a "natural" analytical starting point, whereas Foucault views the body and knowledge about it as "constructed." Foucault, in essence, sees medicine's understanding of the body as historically specific.[8] To apply his work here is thus to redefine the field's basic approach — a notable influence, to say the least. The leading sociologist of health, David Armstrong, has written provocatively about subjectivity within medicine,[9] identity within public health,[10] and the development of medical knowledge,[11] using Foucault's genealogical method.

The influential British sociologist Nikolas Rose* has stayed faithfully within the tradition of Foucault to write about the psychiatric sciences.[12] The sociologists William Ray Arney and Jane Neill have traced the transformation of the understanding of the pain of childbirth, claiming that obstetricians' comprehension of such pain altered alongside changes in the "power-knowledge"*[13] discourses of pain.[14] Deborah Lupton of the University of Canberra argues that public health practices, which are typically taken for granted as a neutral application of science, are in fact value-laden, socially subjective, and context-dependent.[15] Each of these analyses are openly Foucauldian, taking as a starting point both Foucault's methodological approach — genealogy* — and his political-economic treatment of power, surveillance, and subjectivity.

Outside of sociology, Foucault's ideas have shaped the work of urban theorists examining the ways in which citizens inhabit, and move through, the city and the role that surveillance plays in these activities. His beliefs have also influenced the work of queer theorists, who examine institutional efforts to enforce "traditional" values such as marriage to someone of the opposite sex. These studies start from Foucault's premise that all government involves social engineering, and that the enforcement of heterosexuality is part of that project.

Summary

Foucault's enduring insights — that identities are not fixed and that power configurations are contextual — have proven useful tools to scholars across the disciplines. Foucauldian understandings of power, and Foucauldian concepts such as "discipline",* "power-knowledge,"[16] and "surveillance" have enriched the comprehension of power dynamics in various settings. His work provides a powerful bridge for understanding both the meaning of a certain cultural issue (such as the prison), and that issue's political implications.

The originality of Foucault's analysis of the links between the individually constituted person and the social whole continues to provide inspiration for sociology. That academic branch is constantly concerned with a basic epistemological* debate about structure versus agency. And although Foucault's original frame of reference is the West, his theories have been applied in studies of other parts of the world, demonstrating, for example, how illnesses may be linked to discursive regimes — roughly, how we talk about illness — rather than to physical issues.[17]

Finally, Foucault's study of power benefits from its timelessness. *Discipline and Punish* is not an open attack on the exercise of power by any specific group or institution. It is a study of techniques that come into play in relationships between individuals, incorporated by those individuals and embodied in the structure of social interactions. As long as human beings live alongside each other, these issues will remain relevant.

---

1. Michel Foucault, *Discipline and Punish: The Birth of the Prison* (Sheridan, NY: Vintage Books, 1979), 200.

2. Michael Hardt and Antonio Negri, *Empire* (Cambridge, MA: Harvard University Press, 2009): 22.

3. Colin Wilson, "Michel Foucault: Friend or Foe of the Left?" *International Socialism*, March 31, 2008.

4. David M. Berry. *Critical Theory and the Digital* (New York: Bloomsbury: 2014).

5. Cynthia Weber, *International Relations Theory: A Critical Introduction*, 4th edn. (New York: Routledge, 2014). See especially: 88, 140, 149, 231.

6. Ian Marsh and Gaynor Melville, *Crime, Justice and the Media* (New York: Routledge, 2014 [2009]).

7. David Lyon, Theorizing Surveillance (New York: Routledge, 2011 [2006]).

8. David Armstrong, "The Subject and the Social in Medicine: An Appreciation of Michel Foucault," *Sociology of Health & Illness* 7, no. 1 (1985): 111.

9. Armstrong, "Subject and the Social"; David Armstrong, "Foucault and the Sociology of Health and Illness," in *Foucault, Health and Medicine*, ed. Alan Petersen and Robin Bunton (London and New York: Routledge, 1997).

10. David Armstrong, "Public Health Spaces and the Fabrication of Identity," *Sociology* 27, no. 3 (August 1993): 393–410.

11. David Armstrong, *Political Anatomy of the Body: Medical Knowledge in Britain in the Twentieth Century* (Cambridge: Cambridge University Press, 1983).

12. Nikolas Rose, *Governing the Soul: The Shaping of the Private Self* (Florence, KY: Taylor & Francis/Routledge, 1990).

13. Foucault, *Discipline and Punish*, 27.

14. William Ray Arney and Jane Neill, "The Location of Pain in Childbirth: Natural Childbirth and the Transformation of Obstetrics," *Sociology of Health & Illness* 4, no. 1 (1982): 1–24.

15. Deborah Lupton, *The Imperative of Health: Public Health and the Regulated Body* (London; Thousand Oaks, CA: Sage Publications, 1995).

16. Foucault, *Discipline and Punish*, 27.

17. See: Stefan Ecks, "Pharmaceutical Citizenship: Antidepressant Marketing and the Promise of Demarginalization in India," *Anthropology & Medicine* 12, no. 3 (2005): 239–54.

GLOSSARY OF TERMS

1. **Administrative science:** the study of governance, management, or public administration, including the study of policies, how policies are implemented, and how administrative systems are managed.

2. **Algerian War (1954–62):** a war between various anti-colonialist factions of the French colony of Algeria and France. The anti-colonialists wanted to attain independence from French rule. The war occurred on both French and Algerian soil and resulted in several hundred thousand casualties, most of whom were Algerian. It is among the most violent wars in both Algerian and French history, and remains a traumatic memory for both countries.

3. **Anthropology:** the study of human beings and human behavior, and their cultures. The discipline draws on a number of other fields in the physical, biological, and social sciences, and humanities.

4. **Anti-psychiatry:** opposition to conventional psychiatric methods and treatments. Although this stance has been around for two centuries, it gained momentum in the 1960s, when political activists and scholars began to question standard definitions of mental illness, and to query how these were developed.

5. **Archaeology:** the analysis of artifacts and ruins to understand past human activity and the societies from which they came. Foucault used the term in the first half of his career to refer to his approach to historical research: examining traces of past discourses and systems provides a way to understand the processes that have brought us to where we are today.

6. **Bretton Woods:** a system of monetary management that regulated commercial and financial relationships among the major industrial economies of the mid-twentieth century.

7. **Carceral:** of or relating to jails, prisons, and similar institutions.

8. **Carceral continuum:** a term Foucault uses to define modern society's reliance on disciplinary and punitive practices. Not only prisons and reformatories, but schools, factories, offices, and hospitals use carceral methods to enforce their systems. The term "continuum" refers to the differing gradations of punishment that these various institutions inflict on their subjects, all in a bid to create conformity. The continuum's greatest achievement is to have legitimized the power to punish: we take it for granted that teachers, doctors, and employers are

there to judge us.

9. **CCTV (closed-circuit television):** a term used to refer to the use of television cameras to monitor public or private places. It is commonly used in places such as banks, shops, and airports where institutions or governments have an interest in observing the behavior of individuals.

10. **Coercion:** the act of manipulating someone to do something against his or her will.

11. **Colonialism:** the establishment and maintenance of a colony in a territory by a foreign and dominant power. During the European colonial period, lasting from the sixteenth to the twentieth century, European powers established extensive colonies in Asia, Africa, and the Americas, with far-reaching implications.

12. **Communicative rationality:** a term coined by the influential sociologist Jürgen Habermas to refer to the theory that rationality is a product of successful communication between individuals.

13. **Contingency:** a philosophical term used to denote that a particular proposition is not universally or always true, but rather that its truth depends on other factors. When Foucault refers to something as being historically contingent, for example, he means that its occurrence was due to a particular historical context, but also that it could have occurred differently, or not at all.

14. **Criminology:** the study of the causes, nature, definition, and prevention of crime and deviance at both an individual and a societal level.

15. **Cultural studies:** an academic field that examines cultural phenomena such as class structure, ideology, national formations, gender, sexuality, and perceptions of ethnicity through a number of different theoretical approaches, including anthropology, political science, and sociology. Such study is premised on the assumption that culture is not fixed, but rather is a constantly evolving process susceptible to and reflective of broader socioeconomic, political, and historical changes.

16. **Cyberveillance:** the monitoring of an individual or a group's computer or Internet activity, using hardware or software, which may be undertaken by a range of entities, including employers, corporations, and the government.

17. **Dehumanization:** the systematic process of demonizing another person or persons by making them appear less than human, and therefore not deserving of humane treatment. Dehumanization is central to contexts such as war, as it enables one to justify killing, and to systems such as colonialism, as it vindicates the curtailing of human rights and of enforcing that curtailment with violence.

18. **Digital culture/digital culture studies:** new media and new media devices in contemporary culture and the study of them.

19. **Discipline:** as it appears in *Discipline and Punish*, a mechanism by which power is exerted. It is not power itself. Rather, it refers to various ways in which individuals are encouraged to self-regulate, such as the use of timetables, the organization of space, and drills to encourage certain forms of bodily comportment.

20. **Discourse/Discursive practice/discursive regime:** in Foucault's use, a way of speaking that is a product of history and power. Discursive practices are the set of rules that inform the ways of speaking available to the individual in a given time and place. The term "discursive regime" refers to the overlaying of power with ways of speaking such that only certain things can be said and certain things are unsayable.

21. **Econometric:** relating to, or characterized by the application of statistical theory or methods to economic data.

22. **Economics:** an academic field in the social sciences that examines economic systems, structures, policies, and trends and their influence on the production, distribution, and consumption of goods and services.

23. **Emancipation:** the procurement of social, economic, and/or political rights or equality by a previously disenfranchised group.

24. **Enlightenment:** also known as the Age of Reason, the era roughly between 1650 and 1780 when Western European culture and thought progressively came to privilege individualism, reason, and analysis over religious faith. The period was characterized by the view that rational thought could conquer any ambiguity and that logic could solve the world's mysteries.

25. **Epistemology:** a branch of philosophy concerned with the nature of knowledge, which seeks to understand how we "know" what we know.

26. **Existentialism:** a branch of philosophy that holds that the individual — as opposed to society, the state, or religion — is the foundation of meaning, order, and morals.

27. **Feminism:** series of ideologies and movements concerned with equal social, political, cultural, and economic rights for women, including equal rights in the home, workplace, education, and government.

28. **Genealogy:** in literal terms, the study of family lineages and histories. Foucault however uses the term to refer to his historical approach from *Discipline and Punish* onward. He distinguishes it from his previous "archaeological" approach, arguing that although both methods address the history of knowledge systems and discourses, genealogy traces the role that power has played in those systems, and in defining certain things as "true" and others as "false."

29. **Globalization:** a process of integration and interaction among the governments, peoples, and companies of different countries. The process is fueled by international trade and investment, and propelled by information technology.

30. **Governmentality:** term used by Foucault in *Discipline and Punish* and his last work, *History of Sexuality* to define two things: a particular form of administrating populations in modern Europe following the emergence of the nation state and, later, all of the systems and mechanisms used to govern populations and individuals, including forms of self-governance.

31. **History:** an academic field dedicated to the study and interpretation of past events and their meaning, including the study of the discrepancies between different cultures' and different generations' understanding of the same event.

32. **Humanism:** a branch of philosophy that tends to emphasize the importance of a universal humanity and human nature, instead of society or religion, as the font of meaning and morality.

33. **Human resource management:** a branch or department of a company that oversees the discipline and business functioning of its employees (who are known as human resources since they contribute to the output of the company). This

department oversees the skills and qualifications of the company's workforce, and arranges salaries, benefits, and time off.

34. **International relations (IR):** the study of international systems of governance. IR scholars might study the relationships between actors such as states, international organizations, non-governmental organizations (NGOs), and multinational corporations.

35. **Iranian Revolution (1979):** also known as the 1979 Revolution or the Islamic Revolution, the culmination of various uprisings aimed at overthrowing the country's oppressive monarchy, which was viewed by many as a puppet of the West and as overly influenced by Western values. The events began in 1978 at the instigation of the Iranian left and several student movements, and eventually led to the establishment of the Iranian Republic, which looked to distance itself from both the capitalist values of the West and the communist values of the USSR. Foucault was an avid supporter of the Revolution.

36. **Literary studies/criticism:** the evaluation, study, and interpretation of literature.

37. **Marxism:** a cultural, philosophical, socioeconomic, political, and aesthetic movement based on the work of the nineteenth-century political economist Karl Marx. Marxist theorists and writers are concerned with the growth of social inequality under capitalism, and the influence this has on culture and society.

38. **Materialism:** a school of thought that holds that physical matter is the key shaper of society and of historical trends. For example, Karl Marx held that the key catalysts of social change are the changes in the ways people provide for themselves materially.

39. **Media studies:** an academic field that examines the content, cultural effects, and history of new media, and particularly mass media such as television, radio, and cinema. The field combines the approaches of literary criticism and art history (in its analysis of particular forms of media and their content) with those of sociology, political science, and history (in its examination of the sociocultural conditions that gave rise to particular forms of media, and the effects, in turn, that those forms have had on content).

40. **Modernity:** a term used in the humanities and the social sciences to refer to

a period of time, generally understood to stretch from the sixteenth to early twentieth century, marked by a rejection of traditional values.

41. **Neoliberalism:** set of economic policies that encourages economic liberalization, free trade, open markets, privatization, deregulation, and the enhancement of the role of the private sector.

42. **Normalization:** in sociology, term used to refer to the processes by which particular ideas of modes of behavior become common practice. However, Foucault uses the term in relation to institutional power's influence on creating conformity: that is, how disciplinary regimes create conformity among citizens and eradicate eccentricity or errant behavior. The strength of modern disciplinary powers lies in their capacity to exert social control efficiently (expending minimal resources), making people fall into line and follow the rules.

43. **NSA (National Security Agency):** an American governmental agency responsible for the monitoring of information and individuals that may have implications for US national security interests. In 2013, the US whistleblower Edward Snowden controversially released information detailing the extent of the NSA's secret surveillance practices.

44. **Organizational sociology:** branch of sociology that looks at the inner functions of modern organizations, and their broader social role. This might include how institutions divide labor, allocate resources, or respond to change.

45. **Panopticism:** theory that the model of the prison, as encapsulated by the Panopticon and its capacity to make individuals self-regulate, is a model for all power relations in society.

46. **Panopticon:** a concept for a prison advanced by the British social reformer Jeremy Bentham. The structure was designed to permit invisible observation of a large number of inmates by a single prison guard. The belief that they were being watched would lead prisoners to regulate their behavior and effectively govern themselves, making the guard's presence obsolete.

47. **Paris Riots of 1968:** a period of civil unrest marked by strikes by workers, demonstrations, and the occupation of university buildings by students.

48. **Penology:** a branch of criminology that studies the theory and practice of punishment and penal institutions, and their effectiveness.

49. **Phenomenology:** in philosophy, the study of the structures that inform our experience and our consciousness. In psychology, it is the study of subjective experience.

50. **Philosophy:** a field of the humanities that studies fundamental human problems related to reality, knowledge, existence, reason, language, and values.

51. **Political science:** a field of the social sciences that examines government policies and politics, and the dynamics of nation, government, and state.

52. **Poststructuralism:** a field of philosophy that emerged in the 1970s as a response to the perceived rigidity and a historicism of structuralism. Scholars in the field argued that structuralism did not account for the instability of knowledge itself: the very structure of knowledge is a social construct, which means that we can never fully escape the systems we are looking to understand. Poststructuralists argue that all forms of knowledge are contingent upon certain assumptions about what constitutes the truth. In turn, this means that any interpretation of a text, historical event, or idea can be disproven the moment the tenets on which it is premised are called into question. Although Foucault resisted being defined as a poststructuralist, many of his ideas can be seen to fall within this purview.

53. **Power-knowledge:** a term coined by Foucault to denote that knowledge is always constituted by power and power by knowledge; in other words, to "know" someone — to classify them — is to have power over them.

54. **Psychiatry:** a branch of medicine that deals with the study, treatment, and prevention of mental, emotional, or behavioral disorders.

55. **Psychology:** an academic and applied discipline concerning the study and treatment of mental behavior and mental functions.

56. **Queer theory:** a broad field of poststructuralist theory associated with both LGBT (lesbian, gay, bisexual, transgender) studies and women's studies, concerned with inquiry into both what is considered "normal" and supposedly deviant identity categories.

57. **Rationality:** the state of being reasonable — that is, to believe and to act according to one's reasons for believing, and one's reasons for action. Rational thought —

thought based on reason and logic — has been the subject of inquiry among sociologists and philosophers since the Enlightenment.

58. *Le regard* (the gaze): a term used by Foucault to describe the role of visibility in modern systems of knowledge and power. Institutional surveillance — be it by the state, a school administration, hospital staff, prison warden, or company head — enables the normalization of a system's subjects — which is to say, it enforces people within that system to conform to its standards, both in terms of obeying its laws and in acting and thinking the way the system wants. Foucault argues that *le regard* modifies individuals themselves: under institutional surveillance, we become the sum of what we abstain from doing for fear of being seen, judged, or punished.

59. **Sociology:** the academic study of social behavior. The discipline examines the origins and development of social relations, their different modes of organization, and different social institutions.

60. **Sociology of law:** a branch of sociology that looks at the creation and implementation of laws from a theoretical and empirical perspective, and at the role of legal institutions in mediating social relations. Some scholars see it as a subdiscipline of legal studies, or, alternately, as a field that combines elements of sociology and law.

61. **Sociology of punishment:** a branch of sociology that deals specifically with why and how we punish, including the reasons underlying punishment and the implementation of particular forms of punishment and their effects.

62. **Structuralism:** a school of philosophical and sociological thought that gained sway in the 1950s and 1960s partly as a counter to existential humanism. Its main proponents were the anthropologist Claude Lévi-Strauss and the psychoanalyst Jacques Lacan. These scholars argued that human experience, culture, and knowledge are contingent upon larger, underlying ideological, sociocultural, and economic structures: our perception of ourselves, and our understanding of the world, is shaped by specific social constructs. At the time it emerged, it was often viewed as a direct opponent of Marxism. Foucault has been associated with structuralism, but he resisted this classification.

63. **Subjugation:** conquering and gaining control of someone or something and rendering them subordinate.

64. **Surveillance:** monitoring of behavior, usually in order to control, modify, or manipulate it.

65. **Totalltarianism:** a system of government in which the state has complete control over every aspect of society. Nazi Germany is an example of totalitarian states.

66. **Vietnam War (1955–75):** also known as the Second Indochina War, a conflict fought in Laos, Cambodia, and Vietnam between North Vietnam and South Vietnam. It is referred to as a Cold War-era conflict due to the role played by competing global powers.

67. **Welfare state:** a system of social or governmental organization that incorporates the provision of support and promotion of well-being for citizens. Examples of social welfare include public education and universal health care.

◆━━ PEOPLE MENTIONED IN THE TEXT ━━◆

1. **C. Fred Alford (b. 1947)** is a political psychologist who wrote a seminal article critiquing Foucault's account of the workings of prison life.

2. **Louis Althusser (1918–90)** was a French Marxist philosopher who is often associated today with the school of structuralism. However, Althusser was critical of certain aspects of structuralist thought, and spent his life supporting the central tenets of Marxism.

3. **Zygmunt Bauman (1925–2017)** is a Polish sociologist and one of the world's foremost social thinkers. He has written widely on subjects as diffuse as the Holocaust, rationality, modernity, and consumerism. He is professor emeritus of sociology at the University of Leeds.

4. **Simone de Beauvoir (1908–86)** is perhaps the most famous, and influential, feminist philosopher and writer of the twentieth century. She is best known for her writings on feminist existentialism and feminist theory.

5. **Jeremy Bentham (1748–1832)** was a British social reformer who became well-known for his contributions to philosophies of law, his advocacy for the abolition of slavery and the death penalty, and his strong opinions regarding the separation of church and state. His design of the Panopticon prison building, although never realized, had a great influence on later generations of thinkers, including Foucault.

6. **Emile Durkheim (1858–1917)** was a French sociologist and philosopher. He is also generally recognized as the founder of sociology. Durkheim's work was largely concerned with societies' transition into "modernity" — an era characterized by the waning power of the church, new developments in technology, and the growth of cities. He is best known for his study of societal organization, *The Division of Labor in Society (1893)*, and his writings on crime.

7. **Nancy Fraser (b. 1947)** is a political philosopher recognized for her extensive writings on the concept of "justice." She is well-known for being one of the earliest English-speaking academics to do extensive work on Foucauldian thinking.

8. **Jürgen Habermas (b. 1929)** is a highly regarded social scientist and philosopher. He and Foucault clashed over the quality and emancipatory potential

of reason. Habermas has been the strongest defender writing contemporarily of the Enlightenment's faith in reason, standing in stark contrast to Foucault's critique of reason as culturally produced and contingent.

9. **Michael Hardt (b. 1960)** is an American political philosopher and literary theorist known for his collaborations with Antonio Negri on *Empire* (2000) and *Multitude* (2004).

10. **Georg Wilhelm Friedrich Hegel (1770–1831)** was a German philosopher and a major figure in the idealism movement. He became well known for his historicist and realist accounts of reality. His concept of a "system" of integration between mind and nature, subject and object, etc., was one of the first conceptual moves that acknowledged contradictions and oppositions within such a system.

11. **Jean Hyppolite (1907–68)** was a French philosopher and follower of Georg Hegel and the German philosophical movement, and a prominent figure in French thinking in the mid-twentieth century. Foucault studied under him and was profoundly shaped by his ideas on the relationship between history and philosophy.

12. **Karl Marx (1818–83)** was a German political philosopher and economist whose analysis of class relations under capitalism and articulation of a more egalitarian system provided the basis for communism. Together with Friedrich Engels, Marx wrote *The Communist Manifesto* (1848). He articulated his full theory of production and class relations in *Das Kapital* (1867–94).

13. **Maurice Merleau-Ponty (1908–61)** was a French phenomenological philosopher and writer, and the only major philosopher of his time to incorporate descriptive psychology in his work. This influenced later phenomenologists, who went on to use cognitive science and psychology in their studies.

14. **Antonio Negri (b. 1933)** is a prominent Italian Marxist political philosopher and activist. He is most widely known for his collaborations with Michael Hardt on *Empire* (2000) and *Multitude* (2004).

15. **Friedrich Nietzsche (1844–1900)** was a radical German philosopher, philologist, poet, and cultural critic whose writings had a profound influence on Western

philosophy. He is best known for his views on the "death of God," his writings on morality, and his questioning of the objectivity of truth.

16. **Nikolas Rose (b. 1947)** is an influential British social theorist and sociologist who has written on mental health policy and risk, the sociology and history of psychiatry, and the social implications of new psychopharmacological developments in the area of mental health. He is best known for his writings on Foucault and for reviving interest in Foucault's concept of governmentality in the Anglophone world.

17. **Jean-Paul Sartre (1905–80)** was a French existential philosopher, and a leading thinker in the schools of twentieth-century French philosophy and Marxism. His work, including novels and plays, relied heavily on the idea that individuals are "condemned to be free," and that there is no creator.

18. **Edward Snowden (b. 1983)** is an American computer professional known for leaking classified information gathered by the United States National Security Agency (NSA) to the public beginning in June 2013. Snowden's leaks revealed various global surveillance mechanisms operating between the US and other countries in conjunction with several global telecommunications companies, fueling debates about national security versus individual privacy.

19. **Barbara Townley (b. 1954)** is a sociologist and social theorist known for her work on Foucault as well as for her writings in management studies, including the use of performance reviews in higher education, government, and cultural industries.

WORKS CITED

1. Alford, C. Fred. "What Would It Matter if Everything Foucault Said About Prison Were Wrong? *Discipline and Punish* After Twenty Years." *Theory and Society* 29, no. 1 (2000): 125–46. Accessed August 9, 2015. doi: 10.1023/A: 1007014831641.

2. Armstrong, David. "Foucault and the Sociology of Health and Illness." In *Foucault, Health and Medicine*, edited by Alan Petersen and Robin Bunyon. London and New York: Routledge, 1997.

3. ——. *Political Anatomy of the Body: Medical Knowledge in Britain in the Twentieth Century*. Cambridge: Cambridge University Press, 1983.

4. ——. "Public Health Spaces and the Fabrication of Identity." *Sociology* 27, no. 3 (August 1993): 393–410. Accessed August 9, 2015. doi: 10.1177/0038 038593027003004.

5. ——. "The Subject and the Social in Medicine: An Appreciation of Michel Foucault." *Sociology of Health & Illness* 7, no. 1 (1985): 108–117. Accessed August 9, 2015. doi: 10.1111/1467–9566.ep10831391.

6. Arney, William Ray, and Jane Neill. "The Location of Pain in Childbirth: Natural Childbirth and the Transformation of Obstetrics." *Sociology of Health & Illness* 4, no. 1 (1982): 1–24.

7. Ashenden, Samantha, and David Owen. *Foucault Contra Habermas: Recasting the Dialogue Between Genealogy and Critical Theory*. Thousand Oaks, Calif.; London: SAGE, 1999.

8. Bauman, Zygmunt. "On Postmodern Uses of Sex." *Theory, Culture & Society* 15, no. 3 (1998).

9. Berry, David M. *Critical Theory and the Digital*. New York: Bloomsbury: 2014.

10. Braithwaite, John. "What's Wrong with the Sociology of Punishment?" *Theoretical Criminology* 7, no. 1 (February 2003): 5–28. Accessed August 9, 2015. doi: 10.1177/1362480603007001198.

11. Burchell, Graham, Colin Gordon, and Peter Miller, eds. *The Foucault Effect: Studies in Governmentality*. Chicago, IL: University of Chicago Press, 1991.

12. Burrell, Gibson. "Modernism, Post Modernism and Organizational Analysis 2: The Contribution of Michel Foucault." *Organization Studies* 9, no. 2 (April

1988): 221–35. Accessed August 9, 2015. doi: 10.1177/017084068800900205.

13. Chomsky, Noam, and Michel Foucault. *The Chomsky-Foucault Debate*. New York, NY: The New Press, 2006.

14. Durkheim, Emile, and Lewis A. Coser. *The Division of Labor in Society*. New York, NY: Free Press, 1997.

15. Ecks, Stefan. "Pharmaceutical Citizenship: Antidepressant Marketing and the Promise of Demarginalization in India." *Anthropology & Medicine* 12, no. 3 (2005): 239–54. Accessed August 9, 2015. doi: 10.1080/13648470500291360.

16. Eribon, Dider. *Michel Foucault et ses contemporains*. Paris: Fayard, 1994.

17. Faubion, James D. "Toward an Anthropology of Ethics: Foucault and the Pedagogies of Autopoiesis." *Representations* 74, no. 1 (Spring 2001): 83–104.

18. Ferguson, James. *The Anti-politics Machine: Development, Depoliticization, and Bureaucratic Power in Lesotho*. Minneapolis: University of Minnesota Press, 1994.

19. Foucault, Michel. *Discipline and Punish: The Birth of the Prison*. Sheridan, NY: Vintage Books, 1979.

20. ———. "Governmentality." In *The Essential Foucault*, edited by Paul Rabinow and Nikolas Rose. New York and London: The New Press, 2003.

21. ———. *Power/Knowledge: Selected Interviews and Other Writings, 1972–1977*. New York: Random House Digital, 1980.

22. ———. *Security, Territory, Population: Lectures at the Collège de France, 1977–1978*. London and New York: Palgrave MacMillan, 2007.

23. ———. "What Is Enlightenment?" In *The Foucault Effect: Studies in Governmentality*, edited by Graham Burchell, Colin Gordon, and Peter Miller. Chicago, IL: University of Chicago Press, 1991.

24. Nancy Fraser. "From Discipline to Flexibilization? Rereading Foucault in the Shadow of Globalization." *Constellations* 10, no. 2 (2003): 160–71.

25. Garland, David. "Foucault's *Discipline and Punish* — An Exposition and Critique." *Law & Social Inquiry* 11, no. 4 (1986): 847–80. Accessed August 10, 2015. doi: 10.1111/j.1747–4469.1986.tb00270.x.

26. ———. "Frameworks of Inquiry in the Sociology of Punishment." *The British Journal of Sociology* 41, no. 1 (March 1990).

27. Guthman, Julie, and Melanie DuPuis. "Embodying Neoliberalism: Economy, Culture, and the Politics of Fat." *Environment and Planning D: Society and Space* 24, no. 3 (2006): 427–48. Accessed August 10, 2015. doi: 10.1068/d3904.

28. Halperin, David. *Saint Foucault: Towards a Gay Hagiography*. Oxford and New York: Oxford University Press, 1997.

29. Hardt, Michael, and Antonio Negri. *Empire*. Cambridge, MA: Harvard University Press, 2009.

30. Hekman, Susan, ed. *Feminist Interpretations of Michel Foucault*. University Park, PA: Pennsylvania State University Press, 1996.

31. Hunt, Alan, and Gary Wickham. *Foucault and Law: Towards a Sociology of Law as Governance*. Boulder, CO.; London: Pluto Press, 1994.

32. Jessop, Bob. "From Micro-powers to Governmentality: Foucault's Work on Statehood, State Formation, Statecraft and State Power." *Political Geography* 26, no. 1 (January 2007): 34–40. Accessed August 10, 2015. doi: 10.1016/j. polgeo.2006.08.002.

33. Kelly, Michael, Michel Foucault, and Jürgen Habermas. *Critique and Power: Recasting the Foucault/Habermas Debate*. Cambridge, Mass.; London: MIT Press, 1994.

34. Larmour, David H. J., Paul Allen Miller, and Charles Platter. *Rethinking Sexuality: Foucault and Classical Antiquity*. Princeton, NJ: Princeton University Press, 1997.

35. Lemke, Thomas. "An Indigestible Meal? Foucault, Governmentality and State Theory." *Distinktion: Scandinavian Journal of Social Theory* 8, no. 2 (2007): 43–64. Accessed August 10, 2015. doi: 10.1080/1600910X.2007.9672946.

36. ———. "'The Birth of Bio-politics': Michel Foucault's Lecture at the Collège De France on Neo-liberal Governmentality." *Economy and Society* 30, no. 2 (2001). Accessed August 10, 2015. doi: 10.1080/03085140120042271.

37. Lupton, Deborah. *The Imperative of Health: Public Health and the Regulated Body*. London; Thousand Oaks, CA: Sage Publications, 1995.

38. David Lyon. *Theorizing Surveillance*. New York: Routledge, 2011 [2006].

39. Marsh, Ian, and Gaynor Melville. *Crime, Justice and the Media*. New York: Routledge, 2014 [2009].

40. Mathiesen, Thomas. "The Viewer Society: Foucault's Panopticon Revisited." *Theoretical Criminology* 1, no. 2 (1997).

41. Miller, James. *The Passion of Michel Foucault*. Cambridge, MA: Harvard University Press, 1993.

42. Nietzsche, Friedrich Wilhelm. *The Genealogy of Morals*. London and New York: Macmillan, 1897.

43. Rose, Nikolas. *Governing the Soul: The Shaping of the Private Self*. Florence, KY: Taylor & Francis/Routledge, 1990.

44. ——. *Powers of Freedom: Reframing Political Thought*. Cambridge: Cambridge University Press, 1999.

45. Rupp, Jan C. "Michel Foucault, Body Politics and the Rise and Expansion of Modern Anatomy." *Journal of Historical Sociology* 5, no. 1 (1992): 31–60. Accessed August 10, 2015. doi: 10.1111/j.1467–6443.1992.tb00022.x.

46. Savelsberg, Joachim J. "Knowledge, Domination, and Criminal Punishment." *American Journal of Sociology* 99, no. 4 (January 1994): 911–43.

47. Sawicki, Jana. *Disciplining Foucault: Feminism, Power, and the Body*. London: Routledge, 1991.

48. Townley, Barbara. "Foucault, Power/Knowledge, and Its Relevance for Human Resource Management." *The Academy of Management Review* 18, no. 3 (July 1993): 518–45.

49. Weber, Cynthia. *International Relations Theory: A Critical Introduction*, 4th edition. New York: Routledge, 2014.

50. Wilson, Colin. "Michel Foucault: Friend or Foe of the Left?" *International Socialism*, March 31, 2008.

51. Zamindar, Vazira Fazila-Yacoobali. *The Long Partition and the Making of Modern South Asia: Refugees, Boundaries, Histories*. New York, NY; Chichester: Columbia University Press, 2007.

原书作者简介

米歇尔·福柯1926年出生于一个富庶、保守的法国家庭。他从事哲学研究；但是由于身处恐同性恋社会，他的同性恋身份让他感到痛苦，他在二十岁出头时曾自杀未遂，后进入精神病院接受治疗。福柯被视为最重要的现代思想家之一。他对权力、知识和个体建构之间相互作用的相关分析，在诸多学科领域产生了重要影响，其中包括社会学、历史学和哲学领域。福柯于1984年去世，享年57岁。

本书作者简介

梅根·卡尔曼博士是布朗大学社会学系的博士后研究员，主要研究官僚主义的道德和公共利他主义。业余时间里，她在非凡演奏乐队弹奏手风琴，该乐队是罗得岛州普罗维登斯的非正规社团。

拉凯莱·迪尼博士曾就读于剑桥大学、伦敦大学国王学院和伦敦大学学院。她当下的研究方向为现当代英美小说中对生产和消费的表征。她曾执教于剑桥大学和国际教育基金会，现为罗汉普顿大学英语系的讲师。她的首部专著《20世纪小说中的消费主义、浪费和再利用——先锋派的遗产》于2016年由帕尔格雷夫·麦克米兰出版社出版。

世界名著中的批判性思维

《世界思想宝库钥匙丛书》致力于深入浅出地阐释全世界著名思想家的观点，不论是谁、在何处都能了解到，从而推进批判性思维发展。

《世界思想宝库钥匙丛书》与世界顶尖大学的一流学者合作，为一系列学科中最有影响的著作推出新的分析文本，介绍其观点和影响。在这一不断扩展的系列中，每种选入的著作都代表了历经时间考验的思想典范。通过为这些著作提供必要背景、揭示原作者的学术渊源以及说明这些著作所产生的影响，本系列图书希望让读者以新视角看待这些划时代的经典之作。读者应学会思考、运用并挑战这些著作中的观点，而不是简单接受它们。

ABOUT THE AUTHOR OF THE ORIGINAL WORK

Michel Foucault was born in 1926 into a wealthy and conservative French family. He studied philosophy, but being gay in a homophobic society took its toll and after a suicide attempt in his early 20s, he was treated in a psychiatric hospital. Foucault is considered one of the most important modern thinkers. His analyses of the interplay of power, knowledge, and the makeup of the individual are considered key contributions to a wide range of academic fields, including sociology, history, and philosophy. Foucault died in 1984 at the age of 57.

ABOUT THE AUTHORS OF THE ANALYSIS

Dr Meghan Kallman is a Postdoctoral Research Fellow at Brown University, working in the Department of Sociology. Her research focuses on bureaucratized morality and public altruism. In her spare time, she plays accordion in the Extraordinary Rendition Band, a guerilla activist collective in Providence, RI.

Dr Rachele Dini studied at Cambridge, King's College London and University College London. Much of her current work focuses on the representation of production and consumption in modern and contemporary Anglo-American fiction. She has taught at Cambridge and for the Foundation for International Education, and is now Ledturer in English at the University of Roehampton. Her first monograph, *Consumerism, Waste and Re-use in Twentieth-century Fiction: Legacies of the Avant-Garde*, was published by Palgrave Macmillan in 2016.

ABOUT MACAT

GREAT WORKS FOR CRITICAL THINKING

Macat is focused on making the ideas of the world's great thinkers accessible and comprehensible to everybody, everywhere, in ways that promote the development of enhanced critical thinking skills.

It works with leading academics from the world's top universities to produce new analyses that focus on the ideas and the impact of the most influential works ever written across a wide variety of academic disciplines. Each of the works that sit at the heart of its growing library is an enduring example of great thinking. But by setting them in context — and looking at the influences that shaped their authors, as well as the responses they provoked — Macat encourages readers to look at these classics and game-changers with fresh eyes. Readers learn to think, engage and challenge their ideas, rather than simply accepting them.

批判性思维与《规训与惩罚》

首要批判思维技巧：分析

次要批判思维技巧：理性化思维

  米歇尔·福柯是 20 世纪最具创造力的著名思想家之一。他的著作《规训与惩罚》匠心独运，为其他学者提供了极富参考价值的范式。故而该书自发表以来，一直位居学界最具影响力书籍之列。

  福柯旨在考察 17 世纪至 20 世纪监禁形式如何演变。起初仪式性的惩罚是施加于罪犯的肉体，这种台上景观式刑罚随后逐渐演变成台下对犯罪者灵魂的规训。

  福柯的作品以其原创性闻名，《规训与惩罚》一书就涉及福柯最令人信服的几条论断。该书的研究重心主要是在知识和权力之间建立新的联系，由此福柯构想出对"观看""知晓"和"权力"三者关系的新解释——即"看到即为知晓，知晓意味着获得权力"。福柯还细致探讨了杰里米·边沁提出的"全景式监狱"的真正用意——"全景式监狱"是出于应对在有限空间里监禁大批犯人所引发的棘手问题而提出的解决方案，这一方案独特且富有创造力；"全景式监狱"是指围绕高塔而建的环形监狱，隐藏在高塔中的监视人员可以随时监视所有关押犯人，或是营造这种随时监视的假象。正如福柯所点明的，在全景式监狱，囚犯由于担心受罚，即便是在没有监视人员的情况下，也会自发规训自身行为。福柯进一步以此思路反观人们在外部世界的言行，在这个世界中闭路电视和测速相机被明目张胆地安装，用以规训我们的行为。

  福柯对监狱的理解富有独创性，他同时也将监狱与更为宽泛的权力结构联系起来，从而论证所有先前关于监狱的理解都存在误导性，甚至是错误的。在福柯看来，监禁的最终目的既不在于惩罚囚犯，也不在于减少犯罪。监禁的终极目标在于使得违法行为变成国家控制和规约犯罪的一种方式。

CRITICAL THINKING AND *DISCIPLINE AND PUNISH*

- Primary critical thinking skill: ANALYSIS
- Secondary critical thinking skill: REASONING

Michel Foucault is famous as one of the 20th-century's most innovative thinkers — and his work on *Discipline and Punish* was so original and offered models so useful to other scholars that the book now ranks among the most influential academic works ever published.

Foucault's aim is to trace the way in which incarceration was transformed between the seventeenth and twentieth centuries. What started as a spectacle, in which ritual punishments were focused on the prisoner's body, eventually became a matter of the private disciplining of a delinquent soul.

Foucault's work is renowned for its original insights, and *Discipline and Punish* contains several of his most compelling observations. Much of the focus of the book is on making new connections between knowledge and power, leading Foucault to sketch out a new interpretation of the relationship between *voir, savoir* and *pouvoir* — or, 'to see is to know is to have power.' Foucault also dwells in fascinating detail on the true implications of a uniquely creative solution to the problems generated by incarcerating large numbers of criminals in a confined space — Jeremy Bentham's 'panopticon,' a prison constructed around a central tower from which hidden guards might — or might not — be monitoring any given prisoner at any given time. As Foucualt points out, the panopticon creates a prison in which inmates will discipline themselves, for fear of punishment, even when there are no guards present. He goes on to apply this insight to the manner in which all of us behave in the outside world — a world in which CCTV and speed cameras are explicitly designed to modify our behavior.

Foucault's highly original vision of prisons also ties them to broader structures of power, allowing him to argue that all previous conceptions of prison are misleading, even wrong. For Foucault, the ultimate purpose of incarceration is neither to punish inmates, nor to reduce crime. It is to produce delinquency as a way of enabling the state to control and of structure crime.

《世界思想宝库钥匙丛书》简介

《世界思想宝库钥匙丛书》致力于为一系列在各领域产生重大影响的人文社科类经典著作提供独特的学术探讨。每一本读物都不仅仅是原经典著作的内容摘要，而是介绍并深入研究原经典著作的学术渊源、主要观点和历史影响。这一丛书的目的是提供一套学习资料，以促进读者掌握批判性思维，从而更全面、深刻地去理解重要思想。

每一本读物分为3个部分：学术渊源、学术思想和学术影响，每个部分下有4个小节。这些章节旨在从各个方面研究原经典著作及其反响。

由于独特的体例，每一本读物不但易于阅读，而且另有一项优点：所有读物的编排体例相同，读者在进行某个知识层面的调查或研究时可交叉参阅多本该丛书中的相关读物，从而开启跨领域研究的路径。

为了方便阅读，每本读物最后还列出了术语表和人名表（在书中则以星号 * 标记），此外还有参考文献。

《世界思想宝库钥匙丛书》与剑桥大学合作，理清了批判性思维的要点，即如何通过6种技能来进行有效思考。其中3种技能让我们能够理解问题，另3种技能让我们有能力解决问题。这6种技能合称为"批判性思维 PACIER 模式"，它们是：

分析：了解如何建立一个观点；
评估：研究一个观点的优点和缺点；
阐释：对意义所产生的问题加以理解；
创造性思维：提出新的见解，发现新的联系；
解决问题：提出切实有效的解决办法；
理性化思维：创建有说服力的观点。

THE MACAT LIBRARY

The Macat Library is a series of unique academic explorations of seminal works in the humanities and social sciences — books and papers that have had a significant and widely recognised impact on their disciplines. It has been created to serve as much more than just a summary of what lies between the covers of a great book. It illuminates and explores the influences on, ideas of, and impact of that book. Our goal is to offer a learning resource that encourages critical thinking and fosters a better, deeper understanding of important ideas.

Each publication is divided into three Sections: Influences, Ideas, and Impact. Each Section has four Modules. These explore every important facet of the work, and the responses to it.

This Section-Module structure makes a Macat Library book easy to use, but it has another important feature. Because each Macat book is written to the same format, it is possible (and encouraged!) to cross-reference multiple Macat books along the same lines of inquiry or research. This allows the reader to open up interesting interdisciplinary pathways.

To further aid your reading, lists of glossary terms and people mentioned are included at the end of this book (these are indicated by an asterisk [*] throughout) — as well as a list of works cited.

Macat has worked with the University of Cambridge to identify the elements of critical thinking and understand the ways in which six different skills combine to enable effective thinking.

Three allow us to fully understand a problem; three more give us the tools to solve it. Together, these six skills make up the PACIER model of critical thinking. They are:

ANALYSIS — understanding how an argument is built
EVALUATION — exploring the strengths and weaknesses of an argument
INTERPRETATION — understanding issues of meaning
CREATIVE THINKING — coming up with new ideas and fresh connections
PROBLEM-SOLVING — producing strong solutions
REASONING — creating strong arguments

"《世界思想宝库钥匙丛书》提供了独一无二的跨学科学习和研究工具。它介绍那些革新了各自学科研究的经典著作，还邀请全世界一流专家和教育机构进行严谨的分析，为每位读者打开世界顶级教育的大门。"

—— 安德烈亚斯·施莱歇尔，
经济合作与发展组织教育与技能司司长

"《世界思想宝库钥匙丛书》直面大学教育的巨大挑战……他们组建了一支精干而活跃的学者队伍，来推出在研究广度上颇具新意的教学材料。"

—— 布罗尔斯教授、勋爵，剑桥大学前校长

"《世界思想宝库钥匙丛书》的愿景令人赞叹。它通过分析和阐释那些曾深刻影响人类思想以及社会、经济发展的经典文本，提供了新的学习方法。它推动批判性思维，这对于任何社会和经济体来说都是至关重要的。这就是未来的学习方法。"

—— 查尔斯·克拉克阁下，英国前教育大臣

"对于那些影响了各自领域的著作，《世界思想宝库钥匙丛书》能让人们立即了解到围绕那些著作展开的评论性言论，这让该系列图书成为在这些领域从事研究的师生们不可或缺的资源。"

—— 威廉·特朗佐教授，加利福尼亚大学圣地亚哥分校

"Macat offers an amazing first-of-its-kind tool for interdisciplinary learning and research. Its focus on works that transformed their disciplines and its rigorous approach, drawing on the world's leading experts and educational institutions, opens up a world-class education to anyone."

—— Andreas Schleicher, Director for Education and Skills, Organisation for Economic Co-operation and Development

"Macat is taking on some of the major challenges in university education... They have drawn together a strong team of active academics who are producing teaching materials that are novel in the breadth of their approach."

—— Prof Lord Broers, former Vice-Chancellor of the University of Cambridge

"The Macat vision is exceptionally exciting. It focuses upon new modes of learning which analyse and explain seminal texts which have profoundly influenced world thinking and so social and economic development. It promotes the kind of critical thinking which is essential for any society and economy. This is the learning of the future."

—— Rt Hon Charles Clarke, former UK Secretary of State for Education

"The Macat analyses provide immediate access to the critical conversation surrounding the books that have shaped their respective discipline, which will make them an invaluable resource to all of those, students and teachers, working in the field."

—— Prof William Tronzo, University of California at San Diego

♔ The Macat Library
世界思想宝库钥匙丛书

TITLE	中文书名	类别
An Analysis of Arjun Appadurai's *Modernity at Large: Cultural Dimensions of Globalization*	解析阿尔君·阿帕杜莱《消失的现代性：全球化的文化维度》	人类学
An Analysis of Claude Lévi-Strauss's *Structural Anthropology*	解析克劳德·列维-斯特劳斯《结构人类学》	人类学
An Analysis of Marcel Mauss's *The Gift*	解析马塞尔·莫斯《礼物》	人类学
An Analysis of Jared M. Diamond's *Guns, Germs, and Steel: The Fate of Human Societies*	解析贾雷德·M.戴蒙德《枪炮、病菌与钢铁：人类社会的命运》	人类学
An Analysis of Clifford Geertz's *The Interpretation of Cultures*	解析克利福德·格尔茨《文化的解释》	人类学
An Analysis of Philippe Ariès's *Centuries of Childhood: A Social History of Family Life*	解析菲力浦·阿利埃斯《儿童的世纪：旧制度下的儿童和家庭生活》	人类学
An Analysis of W. Chan Kim & Renée Mauborgne's *Blue Ocean Strategy*	解析金伟灿/勒妮·莫博涅《蓝海战略》	商业
An Analysis of John P. Kotter's *Leading Change*	解析约翰·P.科特《领导变革》	商业
An Analysis of Michael E. Porter's *Competitive Strategy: Techniques for Analyzing Industries and Competitors*	解析迈克尔·E.波特《竞争战略：分析产业和竞争对手的技术》	商业
An Analysis of Jean Lave & Etienne Wenger's *Situated Learning: Legitimate Peripheral Participation*	解析琼·莱夫/艾蒂纳·温格《情境学习：合法的边缘性参与》	商业
An Analysis of Douglas McGregor's *The Human Side of Enterprise*	解析道格拉斯·麦格雷戈《企业的人性面》	商业
An Analysis of Milton Friedman's *Capitalism and Freedom*	解析米尔顿·弗里德曼《资本主义与自由》	商业
An Analysis of Ludwig von Mises's *The Theory of Money and Credit*	解析路德维希·冯·米塞斯《货币和信用理论》	经济学
An Analysis of Adam Smith's *The Wealth of Nations*	解析亚当·斯密《国富论》	经济学
An Analysis of Thomas Piketty's *Capital in the Twenty-First Century*	解析托马斯·皮凯蒂《21世纪资本论》	经济学
An Analysis of Nassim Nicholas Taleb's *The Black Swan: The Impact of the Highly Improbable*	解析纳西姆·尼古拉斯·塔勒布《黑天鹅：如何应对不可预知的未来》	经济学
An Analysis of Ha-Joon Chang's *Kicking Away the Ladder*	解析张夏准《富国陷阱：发达国家为何踢开梯子》	经济学
An Analysis of Thomas Robert Malthus's *An Essay on the Principle of Population*	解析托马斯·罗伯特·马尔萨斯《人口论》	经济学

An Analysis of John Maynard Keynes's *The General Theory of Employment, Interest and Money*	解析约翰·梅纳德·凯恩斯《就业、利息和货币通论》	经济学
An Analysis of Milton Friedman's *The Role of Monetary Policy*	解析米尔顿·弗里德曼《货币政策的作用》	经济学
An Analysis of Burton G. Malkiel's *A Random Walk Down Wall Street*	解析伯顿·G.马尔基尔《漫步华尔街》	经济学
An Analysis of Friedrich A. Hayek's *The Road to Serfdom*	解析弗里德里希·A.哈耶克《通往奴役之路》	经济学
An Analysis of Charles P. Kindleberger's *Manias, Panics, and Crashes: A History of Financial Crises*	解析查尔斯·P.金德尔伯格《疯狂、惊恐和崩溃：金融危机史》	经济学
An Analysis of Amartya Sen's *Development as Freedom*	解析阿马蒂亚·森《以自由看待发展》	经济学
An Analysis of Rachel Carson's *Silent Spring*	解析蕾切尔·卡森《寂静的春天》	地理学
An Analysis of Charles Darwin's *On the Origin of Species: by Means of Natural Selection, or The Preservation of Favoured Races in the Struggle for Life*	解析查尔斯·达尔文《物种起源》	地理学
An Analysis of World Commission on Environment and Development's *The Brundtland Report: Our Common Future*	解析世界环境与发展委员会《布伦特兰报告：我们共同的未来》	地理学
An Analysis of James E. Lovelock's *Gaia: A New Look at Life on Earth*	解析詹姆斯·E.拉伍洛克《盖娅：地球生命的新视野》	地理学
An Analysis of Paul Kennedy's *The Rise and Fall of the Great Powers: Economic Change and Military Conflict from 1500–2000*	解析保罗·肯尼迪《大国的兴衰：1500—2000年的经济变革与军事冲突》	历史
An Analysis of Janet L. Abu-Lughod's *Before European Hegemony: The World System A. D. 1250–1350*	解析珍妮特·L.阿布-卢格霍德《欧洲霸权之前：1250—1350年的世界体系》	历史
An Analysis of Alfred W. Crosby's *The Columbian Exchange: Biological and Cultural Consequences of 1492*	解析艾尔弗雷德·W.克罗斯比《哥伦布大交换：1492年以后的生物影响和文化冲击》	历史
An Analysis of Tony Judt's *Postwar: A History of Europe since 1945*	解析托尼·朱特《战后欧洲史》	历史
An Analysis of Richard J. Evans's *In Defence of History*	解析理查德·J.艾文斯《捍卫历史》	历史
An Analysis of Eric Hobsbawm's *The Age of Revolution: Europe 1789–1848*	解析艾瑞克·霍布斯鲍姆《革命的年代：欧洲1789—1848年》	历史

An Analysis of Roland Barthes's *Mythologies*	解析罗兰·巴特《神话学》	文学与批判理论
An Analysis of Simone de Beauvoir's *The Second Sex*	解析西蒙娜·德·波伏娃《第二性》	文学与批判理论
An Analysis of Edward W. Said's *Orientalism*	解析爱德华·W. 萨义德《东方主义》	文学与批判理论
An Analysis of Virginia Woolf's *A Room of One's Own*	解析弗吉尼亚·伍尔芙《一间自己的房间》	文学与批判理论
An Analysis of Judith Butler's *Gender Trouble*	解析朱迪斯·巴特勒《性别麻烦》	文学与批判理论
An Analysis of Ferdinand de Saussure's *Course in General Linguistics*	解析费尔迪南·德·索绪尔《普通语言学教程》	文学与批判理论
An Analysis of Susan Sontag's *On Photography*	解析苏珊·桑塔格《论摄影》	文学与批判理论
An Analysis of Walter Benjamin's *The Work of Art in the Age of Mechanical Reproduction*	解析瓦尔特·本雅明《机械复制时代的艺术作品》	文学与批判理论
An Analysis of W. E. B. Du Bois's *The Souls of Black Folk*	解析 W.E.B. 杜波依斯《黑人的灵魂》	文学与批判理论
An Analysis of Plato's *The Republic*	解析柏拉图《理想国》	哲学
An Analysis of Plato's *Symposium*	解析柏拉图《会饮篇》	哲学
An Analysis of Aristotle's *Metaphysics*	解析亚里士多德《形而上学》	哲学
An Analysis of Aristotle's *Nicomachean Ethics*	解析亚里士多德《尼各马可伦理学》	哲学
An Analysis of Immanuel Kant's *Critique of Pure Reason*	解析伊曼努尔·康德《纯粹理性批判》	哲学
An Analysis of Ludwig Wittgenstein's *Philosophical Investigations*	解析路德维希·维特根斯坦《哲学研究》	哲学
An Analysis of G. W. F. Hegel's *Phenomenology of Spirit*	解析 G. W. F. 黑格尔《精神现象学》	哲学
An Analysis of Baruch Spinoza's *Ethics*	解析巴鲁赫·斯宾诺莎《伦理学》	哲学
An Analysis of Hannah Arendt's *The Human Condition*	解析汉娜·阿伦特《人的境况》	哲学
An Analysis of G. E. M. Anscombe's *Modern Moral Philosophy*	解析 G. E. M. 安斯康姆《现代道德哲学》	哲学
An Analysis of David Hume's *An Enquiry Concerning Human Understanding*	解析大卫·休谟《人类理解研究》	哲学

An Analysis of Søren Kierkegaard's *Fear and Trembling*	解析索伦·克尔凯郭尔《恐惧与战栗》	哲学
An Analysis of René Descartes's *Meditations on First Philosophy*	解析勒内·笛卡尔《第一哲学沉思录》	哲学
An Analysis of Friedrich Nietzsche's *On the Genealogy of Morality*	解析弗里德里希·尼采《论道德的谱系》	哲学
An Analysis of Gilbert Ryle's *The Concept of Mind*	解析吉尔伯特·赖尔《心的概念》	哲学
An Analysis of Thomas Kuhn's *The Structure of Scientific Revolutions*	解析托马斯·库恩《科学革命的结构》	哲学
An Analysis of John Stuart Mill's *Utilitarianism*	解析约翰·斯图亚特·穆勒《功利主义》	哲学
An Analysis of Aristotle's *Politics*	解析亚里士多德《政治学》	政治学
An Analysis of Niccolò Machiavelli's *The Prince*	解析尼科洛·马基雅维利《君主论》	政治学
An Analysis of Karl Marx's *Capital*	解析卡尔·马克思《资本论》	政治学
An Analysis of Benedict Anderson's *Imagined Communities*	解析本尼迪克特·安德森《想象的共同体》	政治学
An Analysis of Samuel P. Huntington's *The Clash of Civilizations and the Remaking of World Order*	解析塞缪尔·P.亨廷顿《文明的冲突与世界秩序的重建》	政治学
An Analysis of Alexis de Tocqueville's *Democracy in America*	解析阿列克西·德·托克维尔《论美国的民主》	政治学
An Analysis of John A. Hobson's *Imperialism: A Study*	解析约翰·A.霍布森《帝国主义》	政治学
An Analysis of Thomas Paine's *Common Sense*	解析托马斯·潘恩《常识》	政治学
An Analysis of John Rawls's *A Theory of Justice*	解析约翰·罗尔斯《正义论》	政治学
An Analysis of Francis Fukuyama's *The End of History and the Last Man*	解析弗朗西斯·福山《历史的终结与最后的人》	政治学
An Analysis of John Locke's *Two Treatises of Government*	解析约翰·洛克《政府论》	政治学
An Analysis of Sun Tzu's *The Art of War*	解析孙武《孙子兵法》	政治学
An Analysis of Henry Kissinger's *World Order: Reflections on the Character of Nations and the Course of History*	解析亨利·基辛格《世界秩序》	政治学
An Analysis of Jean-Jacques Rousseau's *The Social Contract*	解析让-雅克·卢梭《社会契约论》	政治学

An Analysis of Odd Arne Westad's *The Global Cold War: Third World Interventions and the Making of Our Times*	解析文安立《全球冷战：美苏对第三世界的干涉与当代世界的形成》	政治学
An Analysis of Sigmund Freud's *The Interpretation of Dreams*	解析西格蒙德·弗洛伊德《梦的解析》	心理学
An Analysis of William James' *The Principles of Psychology*	解析威廉·詹姆斯《心理学原理》	心理学
An Analysis of Philip Zimbardo's *The Lucifer Effect*	解析菲利普·津巴多《路西法效应》	心理学
An Analysis of Leon Festinger's *A Theory of Cognitive Dissonance*	解析利昂·费斯汀格《认知失调论》	心理学
An Analysis of Richard H. Thaler & Cass R. Sunstein's *Nudge: Improving Decisions about Health, Wealth, and Happiness*	解析理查德·H.泰勒/卡斯·R.桑斯坦《助推：如何做出有关健康、财富和幸福的更优决策》	心理学
An Analysis of Gordon Allport's *The Nature of Prejudice*	解析高尔登·奥尔波特《偏见的本质》	心理学
An Analysis of Steven Pinker's *The Better Angels of Our Nature: Why Violence Has Declined*	解析斯蒂芬·平克《人性中的善良天使：暴力为什么会减少》	心理学
An Analysis of Stanley Milgram's *Obedience to Authority*	解析斯坦利·米尔格拉姆《对权威的服从》	心理学
An Analysis of Betty Friedan's *The Feminine Mystique*	解析贝蒂·弗里丹《女性的奥秘》	心理学
An Analysis of David Riesman's *The Lonely Crowd: A Study of the Changing American Character*	解析大卫·理斯曼《孤独的人群：美国人社会性格演变之研究》	社会学
An Analysis of Franz Boas's *Race, Language and Culture*	解析弗朗兹·博厄斯《种族、语言与文化》	社会学
An Analysis of Pierre Bourdieu's *Outline of a Theory of Practice*	解析皮埃尔·布尔迪厄《实践理论大纲》	社会学
An Analysis of Max Weber's *The Protestant Ethic and the Spirit of Capitalism*	解析马克斯·韦伯《新教伦理与资本主义精神》	社会学
An Analysis of Jane Jacobs's *The Death and Life of Great American Cities*	解析简·雅各布斯《美国大城市的死与生》	社会学
An Analysis of C. Wright Mills's *The Sociological Imagination*	解析C.赖特·米尔斯《社会学的想象力》	社会学
An Analysis of Robert E. Lucas Jr.'s *Why Doesn't Capital Flow from Rich to Poor Countries?*	解析小罗伯特·E.卢卡斯《为何资本不从富国流向穷国？》	社会学

An Analysis of Émile Durkheim's *On Suicide*	解析埃米尔·迪尔凯姆《自杀论》	社会学
An Analysis of Eric Hoffer's *The True Believer: Thoughts on the Nature of Mass Movements*	解析埃里克·霍弗《狂热分子：群众运动圣经》	社会学
An Analysis of Jared M. Diamond's *Collapse: How Societies Choose to Fail or Survive*	解析贾雷德·M.戴蒙德《大崩溃：社会如何选择兴亡》	社会学
An Analysis of Michel Foucault's *The History of Sexuality Vol. 1: The Will to Knowledge*	解析米歇尔·福柯《性史（第一卷）：求知意志》	社会学
An Analysis of Michel Foucault's *Discipline and Punish*	解析米歇尔·福柯《规训与惩罚》	社会学
An Analysis of Richard Dawkins's *The Selfish Gene*	解析理查德·道金斯《自私的基因》	社会学
An Analysis of Antonio Gramsci's *Prison Notebooks*	解析安东尼奥·葛兰西《狱中札记》	社会学
An Analysis of Augustine's *Confessions*	解析奥古斯丁《忏悔录》	神学
An Analysis of C. S. Lewis's *The Abolition of Man*	解析 C. S. 路易斯《人之废》	神学

图书在版编目（CIP）数据

解析米歇尔·福柯《规训与惩罚》：汉、英 / 梅根·卡尔曼（Meghan Kallman），
拉凯莱·迪尼（Rachele Dini）著；余畅译 . —上海：上海外语教育出版社，2020
（世界思想宝库钥匙丛书）
ISBN 978-7-5446-6126-3

Ⅰ . ①解… Ⅱ . ①梅… ②拉… ③余… Ⅲ . ①福柯（Foucault, Michel 1926—1984
哲学思想－研究－汉、英 Ⅳ . ① B565.59

中国版本图书馆 CIP 数据核字（2020）第 014523 号

This Chinese-English bilingual edition of *An Analysis of Michel Foucault's* Discipline and Punish
is published by arrangement with Macat International Limited.
Licensed for sale throughout the world.

本书汉英双语版由 Macat 国际有限公司授权上海外语教育出版社有限公司出版。
供在全世界范围内发行、销售。

图字：09 – 2018 – 549

出版发行：上海外语教育出版社
（上海外国语大学内）　邮编：**200083**
电　　话：021-65425300（总机）
电子邮箱：bookinfo@sflep.com.cn
网　　址：http://www.sflep.com
责任编辑：王　璐

印　　刷：上海信老印刷厂
开　　本：890×1240　1/32　印张 6　字数 124 千字
版　　次：2020 年 8 月第 1 版　2020 年 8 月第 1 次印刷
印　　数：2 100 册

书　　号：ISBN 978-7-5446-6126-3
定　　价：30.00 元
本版图书如有印装质量问题，可向本社调换
质量服务热线：**4008-213-263**　电子邮箱：**editorial@sflep.com**